M000306375

A MAN FROM THE PALATINATE

THE AUTOBIOGRAPHY
OF
JACOB M. YINGLING
(JUENGLING)

THE RYE PRESS, WESTMINSTER, MD

To Fran
a special friend
Jake

Copyright © 2000 by Jacob M. Yingling

All rights reserved. No part of this book shall be reproduced or transmitted in any form or by any means, electronic, mechanical, magnetic, photographic including photocopying, recording or by any information storage and retrieval system, without prior written permission of the publisher. No patent liability is assumed with respect to the use of the information contained herein. Although every precaution has been taken in the preparation of this book, the publisher and author assume no responsibility for errors or omissions. Neither is any liability assumed for damages resulting from the use of the information contained herein.

ISBN 0-7414-0445-1

Published by:

519 West Lancaster Avenue
Haverford, PA 19041-1413
Info@buybooksontheweb.com
www.buybooksontheweb.com
Toll-free (877) BUY BOOK
Local Phone (610) 520-2500
Fax (610) 519-0261

Printed in the United States of America

Printed on Recycled Paper

Published August, 2002

DEDICATION

I dedicate A MAN FROM THE PALATINATE to my wife, Genny, and to my mother, Emma. My autobiography is as much theirs as it is mine. From them came all the good things in my life. Then, to my Father, I need to say, "I thank you for believing in me and supporting me without question except when you wanted to help me face my life's challenges with unfailing good advice.

ACKNOWLEDGEMENTS:

AL BETZ. THE LIFE HISTORIES CENTER,
INITIAL INTERVIEWS AND COMPUTERIZATION

BEATE BUBEL, RYE PRESS
COMPUTERS, GRAPHICS AND PHOTOGRAPHS

DEXTER ROBINSON, RYE PRESS
EDITORIAL DIRECTOR

Published by:
THE RYE PRESS
P.O. BOX 1014
WESTMINSTER, MD. 21158

TABLE OF CONTENTS

FORWARD

The forward contains three commentaries by long time contacts who have known this author for years as well as by his sons. All of us have worked with Jake in one venture or another over long periods of time. In my own case I was closely associated with Jake in a variety of businesses as well as in Annapolis. The simple fact that our friendship has survived many years and many ups and downs speaks well for the on-going friendship.

This book stands as a testimony to a well planned life and to hard work, as well as to the support of dedicated parents. Like all histories the book could have been expressed in either a single word or in tomes. What to exclude is always more of a problem than what to include.

Obviously, Jake kept meticulous records over a long period of time. His personal archives could well serve as a guide to anyone wishing to construct his own family history. It is especially interesting to me to see that someone who graduated from Gettysburg College in the 1950's seems completely comfortable with the new research potential presented by the WEB.

This family history will run on a brand new type of press designed to permit short runs on demand at a reasonable cost.

Dexter Robinson, THE RYE PRESS

So Jake Yingling is writing his autobiography and joining the ranks of Franklin, Cellini and George Burns?– not to mention Abraham Lincoln, George Washington and Franklin D. Roosevelt. (They never wrote autobiographies, so that's why I won't mention them.)

I've known Jake off and on (mostly off) since 1936, when both of us were dressed up and escorted by our loving mothers down the street and around the corner to the same parochial elementary school. It was the first day of First Grade.

We lived on the same street, Jake in the 200 block and I in the 300 block of South Washington Street (In fact I was born in the same row of houses but moved in my infancy). I spent the next 16 or 17 years at number 311 before moving yet again down the street to 347. There was just some wonderful attraction about that street it seemed. I couldn't get off it.

Jake was firmly installed at that 200 block and I at 311 while we went to school together. We played in the same schoolyard, and walked each other back and forth to school on occasion. Neither believed at that time that the world didn't revolve around Gettysburg (which, of course, it did) or that there could ever be any occasion momentous enough to cause us to leave. Our parents were firmly ensconced there, just as their parents and their parents before them, ad infinitum. But as it proved, we were wrong. We did leave.

And of course we were separated even before we left. In the fourth grade I was held back because of a lengthy illness (something about a heart murmur) plus my own laziness. In those days and at that level when you missed your final exam, that was it. No chance to take them over.

So Jake went on ahead of me, on to his life and I on to mine. We would meet on the street at times, but we seldom visited. Of course I never dreamed at the time that Jake would have the ambition and drive to become what he did. Both of us lived on the wrong side of the tracks (literally). North Washington Street was the good side and South Washington the bad one. People on the wrong side were pretty much expected to stay there and become factory workers, tradesmen, or join the ranks of the unemployed.

But Jake didn't settle for that I learned later. He had that energy, that ambition and that perseverance to move on. And though we met in High School at times, we pretty much drifted apart. I went on to my life in Chambersburg and Jake went on to great things. And so the story seemed to end, until one New Year's Day a few years ago when Jake called and asked if I recognized his voice. Well, of course, I could have lied, but then he would have had me, because I couldn't have told him. But I certainly remembered the moment he said 'Jake Yingling'' And then, just like that, the whole web of fifty years growth was swept away and I could picture Jake Yingling at the tender age of bout 8 or 9. It was just as if he were standing there again.

I quickly learned that he had been though all these very successful phases of a well-spent career- teacher, book publisher, assemblyman in the Maryland legislature, banker, and in his own words 'Rainmaker' – all these wonderful things.

So even though I wasn't with you all that time, Jake my heart goes out to you to say, 'Congratulations. You've done pretty well for one of us old South Washington Street kids. And after all these years, I wish you the best.

Marcus Steinour

(EDITOR'S NOTE: I have had a chance to meet with and get to know Marcus well over the past two years. I have been privileged to read some of his writing and even was fortunate enough to attend the staging of one of his plays. Marcus has a delicate touch with dialogue and an infinite concern for the reality of the characters he creates in his plays. He has won acclaim, had his plays staged off Broadway and has been the recipient of national awards. Ever too modest, to proclaim his own success, Marcus, too, can claim to be a very successful escapee from South Washington Street.)

"One of the great pleasures of being the director of a county historical society is working with diverse people, including members, community leaders and the general public. Every new project undertaken by the Society introduces new people some of whom develop long term relationships with our organizations. Jacob M. Yingling was introduced to the Society during a 1992 endowment campaign effort. Like many local people he had known of the Society's work for many years, but was unfamiliar with our rich collections. After using some of the library collections, he quickly became an enthusiastic supporter. He served as President of the Board of Directors from 1993 to 1994. During his presidency, the Society stabilized its financial conditions, renovated two historic properties and accomplished a number of important projects.

"Jake and I shared many conversations about history during his presidency. One memorable occasion was a twenty-four hour road trip to Tiffin, Ohio in a rental truck. We went to pick up a bequest of nineteenth century heirlooms from a Yingling family member. Her ancestors had moved from Taneytown, Carroll County in the 1870's and she wanted the family furnishings to become part of the Society's permanent collection. Jake and I were particularly interested in a gold ring bearing the Yingling coat of arms which we hoped was an early piece. It turned out to be a somewhat disappointing example made in the 1930's. The other items in the bequest more than made up for the minor disappointment and we took great pleasure in bringing it home.

"The long trip provided ample opportunity to talk about personal, family, and community history as well as some philosophic topics. Jake wondered out loud if I thought he should record some of his experiences. I did and happily, some of the stories he shared on that memorable trip are included in this volume."

Jay Graybeal,
Director, Carroll County Historical Society

A TRIBUTE TO OUR FATHER
JACOB M. YINGLING

Dad always maintained strong discipline and was somewhat strict in raising Steve and me. The outgrowth of this was a strong moral sense that my brother and I have tried to exhibit in our professional and family lives. An overriding theme in growing up was 'DO THE RIGHT THING'. Another theme was 'IT'S NOT WHAT YOU ACCOMPLISH IN LIFE, IT'S HOW YOU ACHIEVE IT'.

Dad expected this of his two sons because he expected it of himself. I believe this credo was the greatest legacy that we received from Dad.

Although Dad was never outwardly affectionate, Steve and I were always aware of his deep rooted love for us. He was always the first parent within a group to express how proud he was of his sons. This gave both Steve and me a strong sense of ourselves as we matured.

Lastly, even during times of contrasting views of family strife, Steve and I were always aware that Dad was steadfast in his ability and willingness to respond to our calling.

His words and beliefs are now being passed down to his five grandchildren, all of whom he deeply admires and loves.

RANDY YINGLING

'JAKE'

How many people do you know by the name of Jake? Probably not too many. I'd guess they might be counted on one hand. This makes a 'Jake' special, one of a few, even one of a kind, unique, standing alone, independent, one who follows only one way down the highway of life, unwavering. I suspect you know what I'm driving at.

I believe Jake's Mother, Emma, knew something of this when she gave him the name. It also happened to be the name of her husband. He possessed many of the same traits. Jake was very close to his Mother and Father. His parents epitomized what today's child psychologists preach that young parents should be.

Emma and her Jake's goals were simple. They were to provide for each other and for their children. Family matters always took precedence over material things. No job was too big, too small, too demeaning, but the bottom line was 'to provide'.

My impression of Jake as I was growing up was that he was always very focused. I also recognized a stubborn streak when he made family or business decisions. But I was well cared for. And Jake was a hero to me as a parent should be.

As I grew older, I recognized that our views differed on certain things. But isn't that one of the things that makes life interesting? You become your own person and as you do, you see your parents as their own people too.

In conclusion, I believe that I have taken on a lot of Jake's good traits. These were consistent with who I needed to be as my own personality was molded into the husband and father I've become today. Over the years I've noted a lot of similar 'Jake' traits emerging. That's not surprising, is it? After all, my middle name is 'Jake'.

STEVE YINGLING

PREFACE

The Yingling Family in the United States traces its roots back to 1710 when Christian Yingling (Juengling), the first immigrant bearing the name, may have arrived in Philadelphia. Christian Yingling came to America from an area of Germany known as the Palatinate. The German spelling of the family name had been phonetically pronounced 'Yingling'. Variants of the name included: Jungling, Yengling, Yenglin, Yingland, and even England.

Christian Yingling was one of many 'reformed' Germans who fled Europe to escape both religious persecution and economic distress. The immigrants included mostly Hugenots, Lutherans, and Mennonites. A major cause of discontent stemmed from the terrible conditions which occurred during and after The Thirty Year War, 1618-1648.

"Throughout Germany, 75% of the inhabitants perished from war, pestilence and famine. Sixty-five percent of their homes were destroyed. This was a direct result of religious differences and the political struggles of petty princes.

"After this war, there was a massive invasion of the productive lands bordering the Rhine by the forces of Louis the 14th of France. Major French incursions occurred in 1688, 1695 and again in 1707. **The Palatine was hardest hit.** The Palatine was roughly that area along both sides of the Rhine River between Wartemburg and Alsace." Also heavily impacted were Baden, Darmstadt and Switzerland.

Coincidentally, during the same time span, William Penn had been granted a royal charter for 40,000 square miles of land in the New World. This massive plat was named 'Pennsylvania' in 1681 and Penn set out to find settlers. Heavy recruitment was aimed at the newly desolated areas of the Palatinate.

Immigration began with a first round of settlers arriving in Philadelphia on August 30, 1683. A second group arrived on October 6. All of these first immigrants were Mennonites under the leadership of Francis Pastorius. They settled in a section of Philadelphia still called Germantown. These were quickly followed by Hollander, German, Hugenot and Swiss settlers.

We say that the seeds of Yingling Family Life were sewn in Europe and fertilized by Papal errors, politicians' misdeeds and the blood of futile and murderous wars, many of which were to inflect the New World as well as the Old.

The common chronology of European events having to do with the foundation of America appears in many books and is easily available. The dates and events listed below apply particularly to the movement of my ancestors out of Europe and into the evolving New

1

World. Here, the freedom of religion and politics ultimately prevailed although sometimes still threatened by the futile meanderings of religious fanatics and political charlatans. While in college, I learned from the Dictionary of Social Sciences that the common causes of war are religion and nationalism. Looking at the current disputes between Muslims and Christians, I must say that not much has changed.

I know, in general, that Christian Juengling's move to the New World was motivated by economic opportunity, a desire to build a safe and secure family life in a land not threatened by constant war, and a need to practice his religion in freedom. But those motivations can be attributed to almost any young man undertaking that perilous sail across the Atlantic. Someday, I hope to better understand Christian's personal motives.

Significant Dates and European Events

In 1500 the Pope arbitrarily divides New World between Spain and Portugal.

1501 Burning of books contesting authority of the Church was ordered by Papal Bull. Martin Luther, age 18, surfaces in Erfut.

1502 Columbus' fourth and last voyage. Amerigo Vespucci on second voyage decides South America is not India.

1503 La Casa Contratacion (Colonial Office) founded in Madrid to deal with American affairs.

1508 Pope Julius confirms that the German King automatically becomes the Holy Roman Emperor.

1509 Henry the Eighth of England at 18 becomes King. Start of the slave trade. Bartolomeo de Las Casas, Roman Archbishop of Chiapas, proposes that each Spanish settler should bring a certain number of Negro slaves to the New World.

1512 Martin Luther becomes a Doctor of Divinity.

1515 Vatican prohibits printing of books without imprimatur.

1517 Martin Luther protests the sale of indulgences and posts his 95 theses on the door of the Palast Church in Wittenburg. Thus begins the Reformation in Germany.

1518 Martin Luther refuses to recant.

1519 In his Leipzig disputation with Johann Eck, Luther questions the infallibility of papal decisions. **Ulrich Swingli preaches the Swiss reformation**

1520 Beginnings of Annabaptist movement in Germany under Thomas Munzer.

1521 Luther is imprisoned and begins German translation of Bible.

1522 Luther returns to Wittenburg and completes New Testament.

1524 Swingli abolishes the Catholic Mass in Zurich.

1525 Luther marries former Nun, Kathren von Bura.

1526 Annabaptists settle down as 'Moravian Brothers' in Moravia.
Jews are persecuted in Hungary. Luther offers Mass in German.

1527 Sack of Rome by Imperial Troops with imprisonment of Pope at Castel Sant' Angelo ends Renaissance.

1528 Henry the Eighth explains why he wants to divorce Catherine.

1529 Diet of Speyer the Lutheran minority protests the decisions of the Catholic majority (thus Protestants).

1531 Henry the Eighth is recognized as head of church.

1532–1546 Total political and religious conflict. Rebellion against the Pope. Inquisition and Auto-da-fe. First Protestants burnt at the stake. Martin Luther dies. Henry 8th dies.

The deaths of Martin Luther and Henry 8th slowed down the conflict between Catholics and Protestants but did not end it!!!!!!!

In 1560 Puritanism began in England. The first Calvinist refugees from Flanders settled in England. John Hawkins began the English slave trade. In 1660 there were Calvinist riots in The Netherlands. In 1577 the sixth French War of Religion began, followed by the Eighth French War of Religion in1580.

In 1607 Jamestown, the first English settlement on the American continent was founded.

My family roots, like the roots of the colonization of America, were embedded in the religious and nationalistic conflicts of the 17th century. In summary, they grew in the disputes among the aggressive political powers of Europe. They echoed the distress and economic uncertainty felt by the common man who was dominated by the ruthless autocracies. On their part, there was a constant on-going search for religious freedom and economic opportunity.

Specific influences included the turbulent conditions caused for Christians by the Reformation; the pestilence and famine stemming from the destruction of the Thirty Year War; the invasion of the Rhineland by Louis XIV in 1674, 1678 and 1693; the Edict of Nantes

3

in 1685 rights of the Hugenots; and yet another invasion during the War of the Spanish Succession. It is safe to say that the entire Palatine, including Baden, Darmstadt and Switzerland were all massively impacted by war after war. In the New World the imposition of the Royal Will continued to impact the rights of the common man.

In 1681 Charles I of England granted the land which became Pennsylvania to William Penn in liquidation of a debt owed to Penn's father. This consisted of 40,000 square miles. Penn wanted settlers. His agents advertised in Germany and their song fell on eager ears. The first voyagers arrived in 1683. Fifteen thousand, including Christian Yingling in 1710, had arrived by 1730. By the year 1728, the early arriving, land-seeking Germans settlers had crossed the Susquehanna River and settled in York and Adams Counties from whence they pushed down into Central Maryland.

Why do I dwell on history? I suspect it's a way of complaining that my own brief span will be such a small part of the continuum of the Yingling family that I need to place myself within the entire span in order to grasp any sense of who we are or what we have done. Then, too, there exists an old saw which says: "If you do not understand and study the mistakes of history, you are doomed to repeat them and repeat them and repeat them.

We inherit the history of everything but our own lives. When you accumulate enough years, it is not always easy to look back over your entire life and express total satisfaction with who you have been and what you have accomplished. In all good humor, I repeat another old adage: "If you want to be rich and happy all your life, select your parents with great care!"

Since none of us can do this, most of us accept our lot. We thank God we made it into the world alive and in relatively good health. Too many people I've known did not. Therefore, I remain eternally grateful for the parents I did select and the lot in life I've chosen for myself. Any good things that have happened to me were a blessing. Any bad things were mostly my fault or due to social conditions I could not be expected to control. This is not undue modesty. It is just recognition of the inordinate amount of good fortune with which I have been blessed.

To set the stage, let me acknowledge what I see as the primary influences on my life to date. There was the Stock Market Crash in 1929 followed by the Great Depression of the Thirties. There was World War II in the Forties which was accompanied by and followed by rewarding experiences in a Catholic Elementary School, in Gettysburg High School, then in the Fifties, Gettysburg College. All of these experiences were heavily influenced by both of my parents. Though it seemed unlikely at the time, right from the start, my Father insisted that I plan for College.

This is not to say that I, even with my parent's help, always made the right choice. But I learned early on that I had to make do with what I was handed.

I married while still in college and my wife became a major source of encouragement and understanding. Just as I hope that I influenced and encouraged and helped educate my sons, so they too influenced, encouraged and helped me as I grew and matured with them.

My sons have fully matured earlier than I was able to do. I am sure they will go further and achieve more than I was able to. I hope their children will for them what mine have done for me.

Beyond the family, there were a number of special individuals who contributed to both my business and political lives. I made 'life' plural although, in truth, sometimes my two lives merged. Always, each influenced the other. Beyond these special people, there were many others who played significant roles in my life, too many to mention individually. The truly special ones are mentioned specifically in this book and their roles in my progress documented.

If you want to grossly simplify the situation, just say that I grew up in Gettysburg, Pennsylvania and matured in Westminster, Maryland. Although I've traveled widely, these are the towns holding my roots. My roots are firmly embedded in Civil War Gettysburg and in the rural farmlands surrounding Westminster. You can take the boy out of his home territory, but you can't drive the smell of gun smoke and fertilizer out of the boy. The twin atmospheres of my twin towns hung close about me wherever my path led. And they still do.

Basic Genealogy

I am a member of the national society: **Sons of the American Revolution.** To achieve this distinction, I traced my lineage by the use of birth certificates, marriage records, passports, baptismal papers, tombstone inscriptions, obituary notices, wills, burial records, church and historical society records as well as numerous genealogy books. In addition, my ancestor's military service was traced through Pennsylvania Archives Series E, Vol. 12, page 814, and SAR national numbers 91110 and 84095. The history of my ancestors is much

5

more complicated than is shown by the items needed to prove our American Revolution heritage, but, for the record, the following were submitted and accepted.

I am **Jacob Matthias Yingling.** I was born 30 Sept 1930 in Menallen Twp., Adams County, PA. My wife is **Genevieve Jean Koontz.** She was born 27 Aug 1930 in Knoxlyn, Adams County, PA. We were married 05 April 1951.

I am the son of **Jacob Charles Yingling.** My father was born 25 Sept 1900 in Gettysburg, Adams County, PA. He died on 18 Feb 1973 in Harrisburg Hospital, Dauphin County, PA. His wife was **Emma Bell Grimes.** My mother was born on 14 Dec 1909 in Emmitsburg, Frederick County, MD. They were married 14 April 1926. My mother died in Gettysburg this last November, one month short of her ninetieth birthday.

I am the grandson of **Matthew Matthias Yingling.** He was born 11 Feb 1870 in Graceham, Frederick County, MD. He died 20 Aug 1939, Gettysburg, Adams County, PA. His wife was **Lillie Mae Weikert** who was born 01 Jan 1874, Adams County, PA. She died 1949 in Hanover, York County, PA. They were married 18 Aug 1894 in Gettysburg, Adams County, PA..

I am the Great Grandson of **David M. L. Weikert,** born 29 May 1849, Adams County, PA. He died 07 May 1920, Adams County, PA. His wife was **Mary Rider,** born 21 May 1848 in Adams County, PA. Married 12 July 1870 at Gettysburg, Adams County, PA. I am the Great-Great Grandson of **Jacob Weikert.** Born 22 Mar 1797. York County, PA. Died 12 Aug 1878 in Adams County, PA. His wife was **Sarah Ikes.** Born 08 Mar 1805. Died 18 April 1877, Adams County, PA. Married circa 1780 in York County, PA. I am the Great-Great-Great Grandson of **George Weikert, who fought in the Revolution.**

The reader needs to recognize that the above list does not include many other identified relatives from various families such as the BISHOPS, STOOPS, AND ECKS.

To lay out my own lineage in a more direct way, I will list my mainline Yingling predecessors straight back to the first one to arrive in America. This, of course, was Christian Yingling (Juengling). I feel that anyone who claims a relationship with any of these is a relative of mine.

Jacob Matthias Yingling: I was born 30 Sept 1930.

Jacob Charles Yingling: My father was born 25 Sept 1900. Died 18 Feb 1973.

Matthew Matthias Yingling: Born 11 Feb 1870, Died 20 Aug 1939.

Jacob Yingling: Born circa 1815. Died 15 Sept 1892..

John Yingling III: Born 4 July 1785. Died 25 Jan 1880. He was a veteran of the War of 1812, Battle of North Point.

John Yingling, Jr.: Born circa 1750. Died 11 April 1836. He was a veteran of the Revolutionary War.

John Yingling: Born in 1719. Died in 1774. He was a veteran of the French and Indian War, Maryland Militia, Captain Morris' Company.

Christian Yingling arrived in Philadelphia from the Palatine in 1710. He died 9 Feb 1758. We do not know the date of his birth but we do know he had at least nine identified children. Seven of them were treated equally in his will. John was not nor do we know how Abraham was treated. We do know it was these two who headed west and settled on Pipe Creek land.

To bring the list up to date, my wife and I have two sons: **Stephen Jacob,** born 13 Nov 1951, and **Randall Matthew,** born 7 July 1959.

Stephen married **Cindi Eni** of Medford Lakes, NJ on 23 June 1984. They have three sons: **Christopher Stephen,** 8 Jan 1987, **Timothy Andrew,** 29 Jan 1991, and **Gregory Scott,** 25 Jan 1993.

Randall Matthew married **Marianne Miller** of Cherry Hill, NJ on 23 Jan 1982. They have one son **Tyler Barrett,** 1 July 1985 and one daughter **Randall Morgan,** 23 Sept 1988.

PART ONE:

GROWING UP POOR
   The Bottle Gang
   More About The Wall
SEEING MY DAD IN
   PERSPECTIVE

A. The house where I was born.
B. Aspers is still eleven miles from anywhere. It is surrounded by open country.
C. A tile showing Abe Lincoln made in Aspers

My Grandfather used to commute from Gettysburg to Aspers by train. Now, the tracks remain but the railroad no longer runs and the tile plant where my Dad works has been totally torn down.

GROWING UP POOR

Before I was born, things were going quite well for my family. My Father had a half way decent job and I gather that the entire world felt good about its prospects. However, in 1928, Herbert Hoover was elected to the Presidency and the country began a relentless slide downhill. In 1929, Black Friday hit Wall Street on October 28th. In 1930, just before I was born, the Nazis gained 107 seats in the German Parliament and the last Allied Troops left over from World War I left the Saar.

I was born in Aspers, Pennsylvania at ten o'clock on Tuesday morning, September 30, 1930. I was born at home with Doctor Jones from Bendersville conducting the delivery. Our family lived in the third house up the hill overlooking downtown Aspers. My Father washed me up. He diapered me. Right then, we began bonding. This was a process which continued all his life and, even now, continues in my memory. Never was my Father not there when I needed him.

All I now remember of Aspers is shown in pictures of me in a stroller being walked by my Father. As another part of our bonding, those pictures, obviously, were taken by my Mother. My Father's name was Jacob Charles Yingling and he had married Emma Bell Grimes. My Father was born in Gettysburg in 1900 and my Mother in Emmitsburg in 1909. At the time of my birth, he was 30 and she was 21.

Aspers is ten miles from the Square in Gettysburg and five hundred years from the economic and political maelstrom in which I've lived most of my life. My parents had moved to Aspers in 1929 to work in the tile mill. Three years after I was born, the Depression caught up with Aspers and the tile mill closed. With the mill closed, there was no way for our family to survive in Aspers. My Father and Mother were forced to pack up and move back to Gettysburg.

We found short term shelter with my Father's sister, Aunt Marybelle and her husband, John Bowling. We moved quickly however because the people who owned the property wouldn't let us cook in our third floor quarters. My Father and Mother were able to rent half of a duplex from Mrs. Munsdorf at 229 South Washington Street.

The family stayed there from 1933 until 1951 when my Father purchased a home at 338 Washington Street. My Father died in 1973 but my Mother continued to live there until 1979 when she sold the house.

It's unlikely that anyone not born and raised in the Depression years will ever understand how difficult those times were. The vast part of the population lacked the respectability brought by regular employment. One curious fact about my own growing up years was that I continued bonding with my Father in a way which never could have been possible had he gone off to work everyday – as did my Mother.

Even today, I cringe at the presumptiveness of fools who say women should not work. Had my Mother not taken a slave level job at the local Hospital, we might have starved. I have nothing but admiration and love for my Mother. She was determined to keep her family together and alive no matter what it cost her to do so. And the cost was high. She earned meager wages for twelve hours a day six days a week. She kept one hospital floor clean, worked in the kitchen, and helped serve the meals. A Mrs. Charley cleaned the second floor for the same wages. That was flat pay. The Hospital did not recognize or pay overtime.

Unfortunately, there was no work for my Father at any pay level. He and most of his friends were totally unemployed until Franklin Roosevelt forced the New Deal Acts through a reluctant Congress. Say what you will about FDR, he rescued the country from the economic depths into which it had plunged following the Stock Market Crash of 1929. (In our small world, FDR's greatest achievements were the CCC in 1933, the PWA on 6/16/33 and the WPA on 5/16/35.

As a result of the Depression, we lived on my Mother's scanty earnings until my Father was hired into the WPA. My Father's earnings from various WPA projects were slightly better than my Mother's, but we struggled badly until 1939 when the pre-war construction cycle revived the economy. Their two wages combined kept my earnings free and I was able to save what I earned for college.

Prior to my Father going to work on the WPA, we had dropped six months behind in the rent. My Father felt honor bound to catch up on that debt. He doubled our payments and caught up. Then, he was able to turn his attention to other vital things like food and clothing. I don't remember my parents ever claiming they'd been picked out for special treatment. Whatever else is true of those days, our family was not alone in its poverty.

The entire Third Ward in Gettysburg was filled with people going through the same struggle. Blacks and Whites alike, they all fought the same good fight as best they could. Everyone scrimped and scraped and squirmed around to just stay alive and to avoid getting sick. Even the people who owned the movie house were suffering. They'd let a kid in to see a movie for a handful of potatoes on special occasions. I know now that Gettysburg wasn't unique. The entire country was suffering.

I learned recently about a movie theater on the lower Northside of Pittsburgh where, in those same days, you could get into the movies for a can of food (any kind of food). I was told the canned food was what the theater owners ate in order to protect their own short supply of cash. We were living in a sick and starving country. We all were. Everywhere across the United States people were going to bed hungry. [One radio comedian is reputed to have asked "Have you ever heard the joke about a starving politician? I haven't! I don't know any starving politicians.]

Beyond rent, our family expenses were minimal. We had no hot water in the house except what my Mother heated on the back of the kitchen stove. We had a flush toilet upstairs. It was properly equipped with the ubiquitous Sears Catalogues. Downstairs, we had running cold water in the sink. Other than rent, our main expenses were food and electricity.

Many of our Third Ward neighbors used a handy dandy home invention which prevented the electric meter from recording electrical usage. I don't know whether the wire had a real name. I called it a 'jumper wire'.

You shaped the wire into a 'U' shape and stuck it into the meter. This kept the electrical usage in your house from being recorded. People employed the device whenever they ironed or cranked up an electric washing machine.

South of us, in Carroll County, Maryland, some farmers ran wires from small transformers hidden inside farmhouse walls directly out to the poles. They connected their 'secret wire' to a high voltage line and stole almost all their electricity. Generally, those farmers left only one light and one appliance, such as a refrigerator, connected to the utility company line. I understand they had a large number of farmhouse fires due to the high voltages.

On at least one occasion, a farmer sold his house without advising the purchaser that the transformer and the 'secret wire' existed. One day the living room wall began to smoke. When the 'city' man investigated, he found the transformer buried in the wall behind a mantle fixture. Foolishly, he poked at the exposed connections with a rubber handled screwdriver. The 'city' man was knocked ass over tin cups out through a floor to ceiling front window.

In 1931 the U. S. Senate passed the World War I Veteran's compensation act over Hoover's veto. He still didn't get it despite the riots in Washington and the discontent spread over the entire nation. In 1933 Roosevelt won the Presidency with 472 Electoral College votes. There was famine in the USSR. The Lindbergh baby was kidnapped. There were 13.7 million unemployed in the United States. In 1934 Adolph Hitler became the German Chancellor. The President ordered American banks to close March 6-8. The boycott of Jews in Germany took effect. Prohibition was repealed.

To understand the severity of the situation, all you have to do is study the unemployment figures for the 24 year period from 1920 to 1944.

1920 5.2%   1928 4.2%   1930 8.7%   1932 23,8%
1935 21,7%   1936 16.9%   1938 19,0%   1940 14,6%

1942 4.7%   1944 1.2%

Pause and study the above figures. Looking back from the advantage of age and experience, I believe they show that the country could have very well dissolved into riots and anarchy had not the problem of putting men back to work productively been solved. I am not bent on trashing Roosevelt in quite the same way I've heard some of my Republican friends do. They seem to forget that Hoover had many of the same understandings of the problems, but he seemed unable to act. FDR knew he must tackle the problems immediately. In a sense he felt doing 'anything' was better than doing 'nothing'.

Admire or hate Franklin and Eleanor as you wish, but don't deny the debt of gratitude owed to them by the country. I've listened to his fireside chats with respect. Even now I say: "Right on, Man! Right on!"

The best testimony I can offer to the effect Roosevelt's policies had on my Mother is that even when I first ran for office as a Republican my Father changed his registration to support me, but my Mother told me: "It's a darn good thing you're not running in Pennsylvania or I'd have to vote against you." She remembered well how FDR had saved our collective futures.

I was too young to comprehend any of this in the early Thirties, but I understand now how tight money must have been in our house at that time. Money continued to be tight right up through the years when my Father first went to work for the WPA. Even in '35 and '36 when the men with whom he worked had lunch meat in their buckets or other foods which cost money, my Dad would leave the house at six AM on a freezing morning with six slices of bread spread with molasses.

In those days bread sold for seven cents a loaf and molasses was even cheaper. I'd guess Dad's lunch cost a couple of pennies. He told me many times that the molasses froze in his bucket and cracked when he ate it. That was his lunch. Try frozen molasses sandwiches sometime. When the goo freezes, molasses can crack into sharp shards. They can cut.

Circumstances gradually did improve. When Dad was working for the WPA down in McSherrytown, he found a restaurant where he could buy a bowl of hot soup for ten cents. That made working in the cold on sewer and water lines fairly bearable. Also, my Mother and Father both saved what they could until they accumulated five dollars. That bought ten bushels of potatoes from a local farmer. We took the back seat out of our 1930 Ford, loaded in the potatoes, then carried them home and down to the potato bin in the cellar. Potatoes, as proved true for the Irish at one point in time, became our life preserving food.

We seldom had meat but my Mother was innovative. She'd create a meal by frying flour with what we called 'fryings'. These were drippings off an inexpensive side of bacon. Mom heated the drippings laced flour until it turned real brown, then she added cold water to make brown flour gravy which we poured over bread to make a meal. We also cooked potatoes in that same gravy, cut them into squares so as to create 'cooked and fried potatoes'. Even today I can still remember the exquisite taste of those wonderful cooked fried potatoes smothered in that glorious bacon flavored brown flour gravy. To my young palate this was a feast fit for the King of England.

My Mother canned vegetables from our own garden and put up peaches in season. We used to travel out to pick up drops of peaches in the local orchards. We were charged twenty-five cents a bushel for picked up 'drops'. When we did buy meat, it was ground beef called 'hamburger'. This cost fifteen cents a pound or two pounds for a quarter. I don't remember ever seeing prepackaged meat with a label showing the fat content. You took whatever the butcher was selling. And my Mother was willing to bet it wasn't all beef either.

I remember one time, as money loosened slightly, Mother decided to buy some lunch meat for Daddy's lunch. I went up to Becker's Store and bought ten cents worth of Lebanon Bologna. At that time, you could buy a quarter of a pound for ten cents. I brought it back to the house. I said, not realizing anybody could hear me. "Would I ever love to have a bologna sandwich."

"Emma!" said my Dad. "Tomorrow, make me molasses sandwiches. Jakey can have a bologna sandwich."

Those depression years were tough on families. It was a miracle that as many of them held together as did. Certainly, the parents were called on to make sacrifices far beyond anything that could be called 'reasonable'. But that very fact bonded me to my parents. Even today, when I might be considered by some to be upper middle class and affluent, I can never forget the sacrifices made by my parents for me and for my younger brother, Mark, and my Sister, Ave. The twins were born in 1938 and I was given the honor of naming them.

As I've previously mentioned, during the worst of the Depression, my Father took care of me while my Mother worked. Almost every day, after breakfast, we would go down to the

A. The courthouse wall in Gettysburg.
B. 229 South Washington Street.

Courthouse in Gettysburg and sit on the low wall which ran across the front and around the side of the Courthouse.

That wall was so low I could sit down and have my feet on the sidewalk. This was the meeting place for unemployed men. Here, you could catch up on the news. We couldn't afford the two cents needed to buy a newspaper but someone would have read yesterday's and could recite it's important columns in detail.

It seemed to me that everybody I knew sat on the wall. I remember especially my Grandfather 'Mac', Matthew Matthias Yingling, and my Uncle Clarence. Even though there were no reserved spaces, even if we came late, there was a particular spot where we always sat. The other men always respected that space and shuffled around to make room.

The Bottle Gang

Among the other perch sitters was a group known as 'The Bottle Gang'. Everyday, they pitched in and bought a bottle of 'Sweet Lucy'. I'm not sure now what kind of wine it actually was because they always kept it concealed in a paper bag. The two men I remember best from the 'Sweet Lucy' drinkers differed from the others. They were Mister XXX and Mister YYY. My Dad said Mister XXX came from a real well known family and was a college graduate.

Mister XXX was always well dressed, but he sat on the wall and drank up with all the other members of the group. I don't know why he had to drink 'Sweet Lucy' everyday. Perhaps the expectations placed on him were greater. Perhaps he had more monkeys on his back than those who'd never had anything and expected nothing much from life. Most of the men just sat on the wall and never drank.

Mister YYY was a slightly different case. He was younger than most of the men on the wall. I suspect he drank 'Sweet Lucy' because he liked it. As World War II approached, Mister YYY vanished into the Army. I met him again after the War. He'd married and become a more productive citizen, but he was still deep into John Barleycorn.

Everyday, as we sat on the wall, my Father hoped he'd get lucky and have some work find him. Not frequently enough, but sometimes, it would. Farmers, and other people needing part time laborers, would come and ask who wanted a day's work. The going price was ten to twenty cents an hour. Everybody jumped at the opportunity except the members of the bottle gang.

More About the Wall

One day, a Mister Johns, who had a farm out Steinwher Avenue, which is now a very commercial section of Gettysburg, came and asked if anyone was interested in husking corn. I was five or six at the time, still too young to stay with anyone else, so I went along while Dad husked corn for Mr. Johns. I was happy to be with him and he seemed proud to have me by his side. He always pointed me out to the other men and they always made a point of speaking to me.

The men at the wall had a deep dwelling interest in politics and were constantly critical of politicians. I even remember the election of 1936 even though I was only six at the time. I remember it for a special reason. There was a big political rally up in Arentsville which I attended with my parents. Food was distributed by the Democrats and the local politicians pushed hard for Mister Roosevelt.

Later, political workers came door to door in the Third Ward and tried to get people registered so they could vote. If you agreed, they came around on election day and paid you a dollar to go vote. 'Walking around money' was very much in vogue in 1936. I watched closely as my parents each received their dollars and went to the polls to vote. My Mother and Father were known as honest people. They were paid in advance. Many others only received their dollar after voting.

This was my first exposure to the real political process. This adventure in Democracy fascinated me then and has continued to fascinate me all my life. It drove home to me one simple fact. Some people had time and money enough to do something other than just survive. **This, in fact, was my first really thought-out evidence that the outside world boiled madly while my family merely held on. I found something wrong with that concept.**

This was my Dad on his wedding day, April 24, 1926.

SEEING MY DAD IN PERSPECTIVE

I have already indicated that my Dad and I were very close. This was partly because, with my Sister, Joanna, having passed away before my birth, I was the only child in the family until my twin brother and sister were born eight years later. As close as we were, it was not always easy for me to immediately sense how my Father felt about things. To me, he seemed strong, stoic and stable. These were all qualities to be admired in those unstable times. I learned early on that running around in circles, screaming and waving my arms bought me absolutely nothing.

In fact, looking back, I don't believe I saw my Father cry until I was seventeen years old. He may have shed a private tear at his own father's funeral, or on other similarly sad occasions, but I didn't see him do it if he did. The first tear I saw came when I took a job in the Poconos after High School and boarded a bus to go off to work. This was the summer before I entered East Stroudsburg State College. I will never forget the impact seeing that tear had on me. My Dad took me down to the bus station. He stayed with me and we played a pinball machine together while waiting for the bus. When it arrived and my Dad saw me safely aboard, I looked back out the window and marveled as I saw tears run down his cheeks.

Despite his taciturn ways, I learned a lot from my Father. One thing that impressed me because it wasn't true of many of my friend's parents, was that my Dad never used the 'N' word. Never once did I hear him make a derogatory remark about a black.

One of the incidents I remember best about my early years in Gettysburg was a confrontation that occurred right outside our front window. It was summer and the window was open to let in the air. In those days there was no such thing as air conditioning.

When my Dad heard somebody moaning out on the street, he jumped right up and ran out. There, almost on our steps, was a black man with his throat partially cut open. Later, I heard that he'd gotten in a fight with a woman named Cross and she'd sliced him open. My Dad took the man to the hospital and probably saved his life.

Another point to which I can testify. I never heard my Father swear. When I was older I heard him say 'darn', dash nab it, or some equally innocuous equivalent, but out and out swear? Never!

The only people who ever hit me when I was a kid were other kids or Nuns at school. My Father never gave me a licking or even whammed me. While he was a small man, only about five foot five and 130 pounds, he was powerfully strong. I saw him pick up objects bigger men couldn't budge. He was a country boy and had the farmer's steel tendons and rock hard muscles.

Now, I must say, although my Father had no problems with blacks, he just plain disliked what he called 'Pollocks'. I don't know why in any detail except that when he was 21 he left the farm and moved out to the Pittsburgh area where he hired on in a chain factory. Evidently, the work force was mostly Polish. I don't know if they'd picked on him, fought with him, or what. But I know he ended up with a totally dislike of 'Pollocks'. When my neice went out with a Polish man, Dad referred to him as 'Pete the Pollock'. Naturally, Pete never married my niece.

In the normal course of events, my sister dated a man who had a Polish name. Although he seemed to be a nice enough guy and he was my sister's first real boy friend, my Dad made it evident he just plain didn't want him around.

My Dad was a deeply religious man although you had to know him awfully well to even suspect it. As a little kid, every night at bedtime, we got down on our knees and said our prayers. My Dad gave us an example to follow since he always dropped to his knees and prayed before he turned in. It became a ritual for all of us. We said the 'our father's', holy Mary's, and glory be to God's in good order just as did he.

My Dad never had much to give me but his full love and support. But I also knew how proud he was of my every accomplishment. He said many times how wonderful it was that I could achieve so much when coming from so little. When I was elected to the legislature, he followed my progress with an eagle eye. He did that right up until he died in 1973.

My Dad had been a Democrat all his life, but when I ran and was elected as a Republican, he went down and changed his registration as a gesture of support even though he continued to live in Pennsylvania and had no intention of moving to Maryland.

Occasionally, on a Monday afternoon, Dad would come down to our house in Westminster for a visit, then stay on to attend the evening legislative session in Annapolis with me.

The first time I took him down to Annapolis with me, I said "Dad we're going to have dinner in Annapolis." Dad wasn't exactly poverty stricken in those days, but he still lived frugally. He didn't spend money easily. At any rate, I took him to a nice restaurant which catered to members of the legislature. The price comparatively low for their Prime Rib Special. Dad, however, took one look at the menu and asked: "I don't see it on the menu but can I get a hamburger?"

"Tell you what, Dad. I think I know what you want. Do you want me to order for you?"

"We'll take this." I said to the waiter, pointing at the Prime Rib in such a way that my Father couldn't see what I'd indicated. "This is my Dad." I said out loud to the waiter. Dad got his free.

So out comes this huge Prime Rib complete with baked potato and all the fixings.

"I didn't order this." He said in evident shock.

"It's alright, Dad. I ordered it"

"Jakey. I don't want you to spend your hard earned money on me."

"Dad, I'm going to tell you a secret. It's a bargain. On Monday night, if you order one, you get one free. This isn't costing me anything." Right there his attitude changed and I could tell he enjoyed the daylights out of that prime rib and potato.

So it got to the point where occasionally he'd call me up and say, "Jakey, do you want some company to go down to Annapolis on Monday night? God bless Daddy. That was the way he was.

My Father always attended those evening sessions and paid full attention to every minute of them. He sit up in the balcony and lean over the rail until a State Cop would come over and warn him. "Mr. Yingling, you're going to fall down on top of your son and kill him." That was a joke on the trooper's part, but my Dad always said the same thing in reply.

"That's my boy down there. I want to watch him and see what he's up to." As soon as the Trooper was out of sight, Dad was right back on the rail again.

I don't have anything that was ever written to me by my Father except one postcard in which he mentioned that he'd arranged for me to see a dentist. He'd signed it 'Daddy' and I still have it. If ever there was true love between two men it was that which existed between me and my Father. He was always showing other people articles from the newspapers which mentioned my name.\

"That's my boy," he'd say.

I've never forgotten how my Father and Mother both came down to Westminster on election night the first time I ran for the legislature. They came down and kept the kids because Randy was only two and Steve was just ten. That was in 1962. They also came down for the second election in 1966. In 1970 the kids were old enough to not need a sitter so they didn't come down, but they tracked the election and we found out from Genny's Mom that my Mom called her and said excitedly that "Jakey winded again. Jakey winded again. That may not have been the most grammatical of statements but it was for sure one of the proudest.

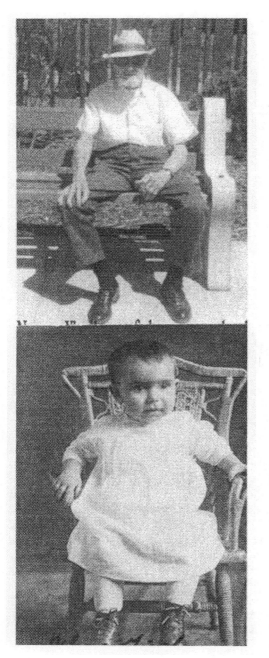

Uncle Norman, my Dad's youngest brother, was a constant in my growing up years.

My older sister Joanna died at 17 months of age due to a medical misdiagnosis.

PART TWO:

WE DIDN'T LIVE ALONE
THE BLACK COMMUNITY NEXT DOOR
WHAT IF THE EMMIGRATION FROM
GERMANY NEVER HAPPENED?

The Thirty Year War

WE DIDN'T LIVE ALONE

The cauldron continued to boil. In 1938 FDR signed the U.S. Neutrality Act but Japan invaded China. A Wall Street Stock decline signaled a serious economic recession. In 1939, FDR sent an appeal to Hitler and Mussolini to plead that they settle European problems amicably. Germany's response was to recall our ambassador. In 1940 Germany invaded Poland and England and France declared war. The cauldron had boiled over even as war spawned construction and manufacture started up an economic recovery.

In the cauldron with my immediate family was our extended family. There were our many, many relatives. Next came the other people who lived in the Third Ward. Then came all the other people who had been displaced and disowned because of the desperate times caused by the Depression. We had not suffered alone. Hard times were faced by almost everyone we knew. Frequently, our family brushed elbows with these others as they too struggled to survive.

One group I first encountered at age eight were members of the Civilian Conservation Corps. The CCC Camp in Gettysburg was located out on West Confederate Avenue. It housed members from Pennsylvania, the eastern shore of Maryland, and a lesser number from Delaware. These were all young black men ages eighteen to twenty. The CCC workers were easy to recognize. They wore dark green uniforms and, to my young eyes, seemed well fed.

These men did good things for Gettysburg. They worked on the Battlefield roads. They improved the Battlefield sites. Indeed, they made a tremendous contribution to the future of Gettysburg as a tourist attraction. It seems a shame that, to the best of my knowledge, no recognition has been given to those hard working young men.

My special attachment to those CCC men, I guess, stemmed from their having helped me save a few pennies during a three year period, ages eight to ten. Mister John Becker, who as the son of Mrs. Becker who owned a store up the street from where we lived, was from Westminster. But he operated a business out of the second floor of his mother's store. When his own children were in school in Westminster and not available to help him, he'd call on me to fill in.

"Hey, Jakey." He'd say. "Would you like to earn a nickel?" Believe me, for a little kid to save a nickel in 1938 was a big time thrill.

With my eager agreement, Mister Becker would put me in his car and drive out to the CCC Camp. There, we'd gather up all the dirty, sweaty uniforms and wool outer clothing from the young black men. I remember holding out my arms as Mister Becker walked up and down through the dorms making his collections. When I was buried beneath a load, I'd put them in his car and come back for another.

Mister Becker didn't own a laundry or a dry cleaning establishment but he evidently had an arrangement with somebody who did. He'd gather up the clothes, have them cleaned, then bring them back and either deliver them to the camp or to the store for pickup. Mostly, he paid me a nickel a day, but sometimes, when he didn't have any money, he'd give me two pieces of candy from his mother's store.

My work with John Becker led directly to Mrs. Becker hiring me to help out in her store. Mrs. Becker was very old. Her husband had been a Civil War veteran. He had died many years before. He had been much older than Mrs. Becker when they married and was dead long before I first worked for her as a clerk.

After supper at my house, I would go to the store at five or six and stay until she closed at about eight. I sometimes stayed overnight in the spare bedroom. For working that evening and staying overnight, I received two 'V' nickels. The 'V' nickels were still around in 1938 although the Jefferson nickels were coming in. I saved those nickels. Along with what I received from John Becker, they were the start of my college fund.

Even though my parents realized from day one that they could never afford to send me to college, my Dad declared early on: "Jakey, you should go to college." My Dad felt strongly that college could guarantee success. Both he and my Mother wanted me to understand the importance of this.

There was one other thing you should know about Mrs. Becker. God rest her soul! She was a very giving lady. Many people came in during the Depression and bought 'on the book'. Some of them never paid her back. In this sense she subsidized a lot of our neighbors.

Her primary stock consisted of cookies, candy, some canned foods, cigarettes and coal oil (an early form of kerosene). She sold this by the gallon. The store stock was painfully sparse. The only meat she sold was Lebanon Bologna.

Mrs. Becker did not have any way to preserve food except in an old icebox in which she kept milk. One ritual I always looked forward to came at the end of the day. It was sharing a soft drink with Mrs. Becker. We'd split a bottle of ginger ale. It sold for a nickel. She'd look into the cookie case before we drank it to see if any of the large sugar cookies, which sold for a penny or two each, were day old. If they were, the day old cookies became part of our evening treat. I think Mrs. Becker looked forward to this financial indiscretion as much as I did.

THE BLACK COMMUNITY NEXT DOOR

Both the Gettysburg Public Schools and the Private School (Catholic) were integrated. Therefore, from the first grade through High School, I attended school with black kids. In truth, I never felt there was any problem with the black community in Gettysburg. But I wasn't black so maybe I just didn't understand an evident truth.

I never realized what a disadvantage there was to growing up black at that time in that place. I don't think I realized the segregation my black friends would experience as they grew up. Against that, not I, nor any of the people I associated with in the Third Ward, certainly not my parents, ever showed any visible signs of racial prejudice.

I lived in the middle of South Washington Street. Right around the corner on West High Street were a few black families. From there on, from Becker's Store up to Breckenridge Street and around the corner on Breckenridge Street itself was where the black community of Gettysburg lived. Ii don't recall that there were any black families in the First or Second Wards. They were all concentrated in the Third Ward. Black families lived less than six houses from me.

One friend I remember from the black community was Jimmy Roberts. Jimmy was one of the first people from our block I knew to graduate from High School. I, myself, was the second. And the two of us, to the best of my memory, were the only two from our block who went on to college.

Jimmy was also known as 'Bolo'. How he got that name I don't know, but Bolo and I played together as kids. Jimmy was always a sharp dresser. He had two beautiful sisters who also dressed exceedingly well. As I recall, his mother worked as a 'day lady' for people. Jimmy's father owned a garage at the back of their yard. On the second floor of the garage, Jimmy's Daddy had a nice pool room where black men gathered for recreation – and probably a touch of the old rotgut. In those days, black men would not enter a bar in Gettysburg. They wouldn't be seated. I realize now that Gettysburg, while nominally integrated, was not at all integrated.

Aside from the garage and the pool room, I don't really know what Jimmy's Dad did to earn money. I don't think he had a regular job. But he had a nice car and they all dressed well. The Roberts Family always seemed to have more, even during the Depression, than we ever had.

Beyond the Roberts, there were several other blacks in the community I felt sure had money. While I have no idea what many of them did for a living, I do know two of them worked as bellhops down at the Hotel. In the Thirties and early Forties, a white man would never work as a bellhop in a hotel. But these men did and they had steady jobs. I have to guess they were better paying jobs than my Father or any of his friends had.

Many of the Gettysburg blacks owned their own homes. At that time we did not. Although I always thought of them as being better off than my own family, this was a random, unreasoned thought, not envy.

Partly, my feelings about the blacks were because my Father had a special friend in that community. This man was Jim Moss, a Constable. Jim was six foot four or larger. He looked like a guy who should be wearing a six shooter and a Stetson. Jim should always be envisioned as high up on a horse. To me, Jim Moss was both powerful and extraordinarily kind. Besides, he was a friend of my Dad's. What better credentials could any man possibly have?

As I write about the black community, I can see in retrospect what I felt about it. While there were indeed some people in that community you could label the same way you do 'white trash', I came to know far more who over the years proved themselves to be good people. Even the black women who didn't have husbands, or had no account husbands, raised their children with an iron fist. They made their children grow up carrying a sense of responsibility.

When I look back I see the black men and women whose families stayed intact as having a special air about them. They walked with their heads up. There were human beings with class. They moved with dignity and I'm proud to have known them.

Jimmy Roberts had a close friend named Joe Howard. Joe Howard lived catercornered across the street from Bolo. As a kid, one of the games we played was called softball, or 'mushball'. Also, up in the field back of our house, we also played football. We tackled in our clothes. We got black eyes. We beat each other up. On the other hand, I didn't know many kids who played basketball. That's except Bolo and Joe and I really don't remember where it was that they shot around.

Joe Howard was almost three years ahead of me in grammar school. Later, when he was in eighth grade, his parents moved out west to Chambersburg. Joe became a championship basketball player in Chambersburg. His school won the district championship and Joe received a lot of press coverage. I was a freshman in High School when he was a senior and I only got to see him play one game that year. I still marvel that someone I played sandlot ball with was that good. He was so good that he was offered a college scholarship. But I doubt that he could afford to accept it.

I've always understood that Joe went directly into the service after High School. I also know that he played in a semi-pro basketball league after the war. I learned later that Joe Howard continued to play basketball right up into his sixties. He was good. Had basketball enjoyed the wide spread pro status then that it did much later, he, undoubtedly, would have been given a shot at the big time. Joe Howard died a couple of years ago in Hagerstown. He was too good too soon for his own good.

That reminds me of another Joe, Joe Carter. He too lived in the neighborhood. I caught up with Joe Carter in 8th grade. At the time I was 13 and he was 17. That was because, like me, Joe had attended the Catholic School. Like most kids, he'd flunked a grade or two. The Nuns flunked everybody several times. As a point of curious fact, I was the only boy I know of from the neighborhood who never flunked a grade.

As I recall, Joe didn't give much of a damn for school. He could read and write, but all he did was sit in the back of the room and wait for the class to end so he could get out and about. I don't exactly recall but I think he went into the service right from 8th grade.

Joe had two brothers, Ben and Bill. Ben was an amateur boxer. Both brothers preceded Joe into service. Their parents were among the few blacks in town who were Catholic. One day, Joe's Dad failed to pick him up as he usually did, so I invited Joe to come on over to our place. It was getting near to supper time, and I hated to see him standing there just waiting. Mom was already cooking supper when we walked in.

"Mom." I asked. "What are we having for supper?"

"I'm just throwing stuff together."

"Well, is it alright if Joe here eats with us?"

Right then, my Dad came home. He reached out and shook hands with Joe.

"Joe," he said. "It's nice to see you. Grab a chair. Sit down. Eat with us."

To my parents it didn't matter a tinker's dam that Joe was black. But it did matter to them that he have dinner with us. I realized much later that my Father knew as much or more about every kid in the neighborhood, white or black, as their parents did. Mrs. Clinton made quite a stir with her theory that it takes a village to raise a kid. My Dad felt that every adult in the Third Ward, including himself, was responsible for every kid living there. I was not aware of gangs or race riots in those days. Maybe the adults cared more. I just don't know, but it was true that with all our money problems there was almost no juvenile crime.

In the early eighties, after I'd left Gettysburg, my Mother went back to work in the Hospital. Joe Carter was working there then,. He would always ask my Mother about me and they'd talk about what I was doing. "Tell you true, Miz Yingling. Jake's alright. I'm real proud to say I know him." Whenever Mom would relay this to me, I always meant to go by the Hospital and look Joe up, but I got busy I guess. I truly regret that. Joe died a year or so back.

I did find a chance to talk with Joe's sister, Esther. I remembered her from school just like I did Joe. Difference was that Esther was smart as a whip and always carried herself with that innate dignity I'd previously mentioned while talking about some of our neighbors. And it didn't come from having money. The Carters were poor, poor as dirt, maybe even poorer than my own family.

I don't know Esther's married name, but I do know she married and had children. I never heard of a divorce or a separation so I suspect she's still in her first marriage. In the Third Ward that was not all that common. Marital relations during the depression were considerably more fluid and less formal than they tend to be now.

In those early years in the Third Ward, I don't recall hearing about anybody actually getting a divorce. Divorces cost money, and nobody had enough to afford one. If either party wanted to leave the marriage they just left. If a woman took a man for everything he had, she'd get nothing. And suing for child support was a total waste of time. Who could afford a lawyer or court costs. Mostly, taking care of kids was by mutual agreement without government or legal pressures.

On the other hand, there was one term I heard frequently. "She's his **housekeeper**."

There were lots of men in the Third Ward who had housekeepers, and there were a lot of women who became housekeepers. If the kids were grown or were not a problem, and there was a guy down the street who had a few bucks, why not? Of course they slept together. I never heard of anybody getting his or her bowels in an uproar over this naked necessity, nor was anyone ever shot because of it.

It happened in my own family. My grandparents separated and my grandmother moved in with a guy from New Oxford. He'd advertised for a housekeeper and she answered the ad. As one result of this, I even shared a room with my grandfather for a time.

Later when my grandfather was at the point of death, they called my grandmother and she traveled down from New Oxford to see him. I was in the room with my grandfather when he died. I was just eight, almost nine, and this was quite an experience for me. At the time, he was living in a rooming house. He'd had a stroke. Since nobody could afford to take him to the Hospital, my Aunt took him in. His name was Matthew Matthias Yingling and he was called 'Mac'.

I was sitting with him when my grandmother arrived. He didn't smoke but she did. So we sat there and I watched as she smoked and they made their peace. Whatever that meant! I don't know which one of them said it, but in retrospect, it was one hell of a line. "Let's have a cigarette together." They both smoked while I entertained visions of

Indians with their peace pipes. I knew the two of them had not spoken directly to each other in years. Nor, after that one agreement to smoke, did they now.

My Dad never took sides between them. He loved both his parents without question. Both were welcome at our house, but they never visited together. If my grandmother was there, my grandfather would just walk right on through the house and out the back door. What I remember is that both of my grandparents were wonderful people.

Whatever was amiss between them never affected the way they treated my parents or us kids. Grandfather had gradually lost his eyesight and was almost completely blind when he died. I still have the cane I inherited from him. He'd gotten it when he received the pension for being blind in 1938.

After my grandparents separated, their house was signed over to my Father and he eventually sold it and split the funds from the sale evenly between the two of them.

I guess that today you would characterize what they underwent as a 'mid-life crisis. Whatever it was, World War II changed such situations into more a question of 'money' then discontent and separation. Once there was money to be made from divorces the lawyers took over.

A. 'Jakey' with Grandfather 'Mac' at about age one.
B. 'Jakey' in the cabbage patch wearing a special cowboy outfit Emma bought from a catalog.
C. Jake all dressed up and ready for school.

31

Great Grandfather David L.M. Weikert (1911)

Great Grandmother Mary Rider Weikert
Wife of David Weikert

Great Grandfather and Grandmother Weikert.

My Mother's Parents: Daniel Joseph & Harriet Grimes.

My Mother's Grandfather, Joseph Grimes, and her Grandmother Susan Anna Grimes.

The Daniel Joseph Grimes Family. Emma is the first
girl in the first row.

WHAT IF THE EMIGRATION FROM
GERMANY NEVER HAPPENED?

I have not yet done, and probably never will do, the intensive research needed to permit any type of definitive answer to this question. However, I feel the question is worth addressing before we move too far from my early years in Gettysburg.

First of all, had not Christian Yingling chosen to come to America, but still married and had children, the Yingling family would have developed in Germany with all of the consequences attendant on that fact.

Secondly, had Christian's arrival been an isolated event instead of part and parcel of a large-scale movement, his reception and growth in the New World would have been considerably different. He was one of a large number of German speaking immigrants and a dedicated Lutheran. Both of these facts speak of comfort and support which otherwise would not have been available.

We are not sure exactly where Christian came from in Germany, but we can make an educated guess. As to his having been German, our best evidence is that this is the language in which he wrote his will. As to his having been Lutheran, he is listed among the settlers who contributed to the construction of the Augustus Lutheran Church at Trappe, PA. This is the oldest unaltered Lutheran Church structure in the U.S.A. It was begun in 1743 and completed in 1745.

To keep this situation simple, let us presume that there were three primary reasons for Christian Yingling taking passage on that ship in 1710,

First, we believe that he came from the Palatinate, a section of Germany which was virtually destroyed. It was initially desolated by the battles of the Thirty Year War, then ultimately turned to rubble by the depredations of Louis XIV of France.

Second, persecution of the 'Reformed Churches' by the Catholic Church had made practicing any protestant religion freely a sometimes thing subject to all types of retribution.

Third, William and Thomas Penn offered an opportunity to gain access to virtually unlimited land to those who chose to become 'settlers'. The Penn agents deliberately sought settlers from the Rhine region because of the economic distress and religious persecution existing there.

It is axiomatic that our schools spend little time on the history of Europe even though it is difficult to interpret our own country's founding in light of anything else. Just as we will later think about how the crash of our stock market impacted the growth of Hitler in Germany, so we need to think about how conditions in 17th and early 18th century Europe impacted the very founding of the United States.

Even as a history major in college, I found scant time given to our European roots. As a child I attended a Catholic School which stills sang hymns in German and offered the Tridentine Mass in Latin. As an Altar Boy I memorized all of the Latin responses and felt a deep kinship with my German ancestors.

In short, if we had studied the Thirty Year War in school,, we would have learned that it took place from 1618 to 1648 and was the most devastating and terrible conflict ever to occur in Europe. Throughout Germany, seventy-five percent of the population perished from war, pestilence and famine. Sixty-five percent of the houses were destroyed.

The war concerned religious differences and the struggles of petty princes for control of the land. To understand the impact of the conflict, just consider the list of formal battles which wasted Germany during the course of the war.

1618-1629 Phase One: Loss of the Palatine and Collapse of German Protestantism.

1620   Battle of White Mountain. Bohemian rebellion ended and the conquest of the Palatine enabled.

1626   Battle of Luter compels withdrawal of Denmark

1629   Peace of Lubeck

1630–1645 Phase Two: Restoration of Protestantism by Sweden

1631   Battle of Breitenfeld restores Protestant fortunes and is the turning point of the war. Sack of Magdeburg.

1632   Battle of Lutzen. Victory, but death of Gustavus Adolphus. Leads indirectly to assassination of Wallenstein in Feb., 1634.

1634   Battle of Nordinger undoes the work of Sweden. War becomes one of exhaustion between France, Sweden and Bavarian Imperialists. Disease and starvation throughout Germany. End of Religious phases of the war.

1635   Peace of Prague.

1634-8 Phase III: Intervention of France.

1634-9 Five years of negotiation.

1635   French ally with Dutch against Spain. This begins the Dutch War of Independence.

1643	Battle of Bocroi. Conde destroys the remnants of Spanish military prestige.
1648	Battle of Susmarshausen. Turenne and Wrangel defeat Imperialists and Bavarians. Battle of Lens. Conde defeats the Spanish.
	Also in 1648, the Treaty of Westphalia ends The Thirty Year War. Munser ends the Spanish Dutch War.

But it didn't stop there. With 75% of the German population already decimated and a large percentage of the house gone, the economy devastated and no chance to plant crops, hunger and disease became endemic. Then came more wars.

From 1643 – 1715 the troops of Louis XIV levied death and destruction over many of the same towns. In 1688 the French troops once again devastated the Palatinate. Following that, the War of the Spanish Succession even spread to the New World during 1701-14.

To demonstrate the destruction visited on Germany, let us consider the results of just two of the many battles which raged throughout Germany during the Thirty Year War. When you consider these battles remember that many historians have proclaimed that nationalism and religion are the primary causes of war. Remember that there are always prosecutors, submittors, and protestors. It is customary for both the prosecutors and the protestors to run rough shod over the submittors. Unfortunately, time has proven that anyone caught in the middle must join one side or the other or be killed.

The Battle of Breitenfeld
17 September 1631

Breitenfeld is five miles north of Leipzig, Germany. The combatants were a Protestant Army under the command of King Augustus Adolphus Vasa of Sweden and the Elector of Saxony. These two jointly commanded an army of 36-40,000 Swedes and Saxons with 60-70 guns. The Imperial Catholic Army was under the command of John di Tilly with 32,000 men and 30 guns.

The Protestants aimed to capture Leipzig.

The casualties for the Protestants included 4,000 killed or wounded, ten percent of their forces. The casualties for the Imperialists included 7,000 killed or wounded and 6,000 taken prisoner, or at least one-third of their forces. The obvious victors were the Protestants and Leipzig fell into their hands.

The Battle of Lutzen
16 November 1632

Lutzen is fifteen miles southwest of Leipzig. The combatants were a Protestant army under the command of Gustavus Adolphus Vasa. It numbered 16-19,000. The opposing Imperial army was under the command of Albrect Wallenstein. It numbered 15-20,000 infantry and 8-10,000 calvary.

The Imperial Army wished to cut the Protestants off from the Baltic and force the Saxons to abandon the Swedes. Casualties included 5,000 for the Protestants and 6,000 for the Imperialists. Once again the Protestants won but the death of Gustavus Adolphus cost them their best general..

I believe that my first two reasons for Christian Juengling to leave his native Germany and risk the voyage to the Colonies are demonstrated.(2) He was a Lutheran and his total Germanic environment had been devastated by war. In 1618 Germany had a population of 17,000,000. By 1648 this had shrunk to under 8,000,000. There could have been little hope for an ordinary citizen who remained in the Palatine without an effective sponsor.

It was Karl Marx who said: "Religion is the opium of the people."

It was William Penn who said: "It is a reproach to religion and government to suffer so much poverty and excess."

A third statement with which William Penn had to agree was made by George Fox, founder of the Quakers in 1648. in 1651 when he rejected a captaincy in the Army of the Commonwealth against the forces of the king. He stated: "I told them that I lived in the virtue of that life and power that took away the occasion of all wars." From the time William Penn became a Quaker, he was completely dedicated to ideas of peace and giving help to his fellowman. This was totally out of context with the war-like attitudes of his contemporary aristocratic friends.

Thomas Penn and his agents undoubtedly echoed Fox's sentiments along with promises of land, freedom and a new start for all of the oppressed Germans they recruited for the voyage to a fresh beginning in the New World. It does seem ironic that the people most upset by the arrival of German refugees were the Philadelphia Quakers who had indeed endorsed the recruitment effort. I suspect they had not anticipated so hearty a response.

Despite the immediate settlement in 'Germantown' of many refugees, most were channeled out into the west and onto the frontier where there were still Indians to fight. But this was also where opportunities would exist for years. This is not the place or time, but I am sure just showing the migration of my own family west to California amply demonstrates this move.

After William Penn was awarded Pennsylvania by King Charles II, he wrote two pamphlets, both in 1681: *A Brief Account and Some Account of the Province of Pennsylvania.*. These were probably the most widely distributed and effective real estate prospectuses' ever offered. Penn's friend, chief land agent and recruiter, Benjamin Furley, who was headquartered in Rotterdam, was in touch with intellectuals and liberal politicians throughout Europe. He saw that the brochures were distributed in England, Wales and Ireland, then in translation in the Netherlands, Western Germany and France.

The brochures echoed Penn's pleas for pacifism, toleration, reasonable and simple religion as well as ordinary human rights and dignity.

The support Penn received from famous shapers of public opinion such as Voltaire, John Locke and Montesquieu assured that every person in the western world who could read knew something about the virtues of life in Pennsylvania. "William Penn could boast of having brought to the world that golden age of which men talk so much and which probably has never existed anywhere except in Pennsylvania." Montesqjuieu also wrote that Penn was the greatest lawgiver since classical antiquity.

To the war ravaged Germans of the Palatine, this must have sounded like a proclamation of a heaven to be found on earth. While it is not appropriate to detail too much political history in this part of my story, William Penn's reputation was greatly enhanced by the sending of Benjamin Franklin to Paris in 1777 as the representative of the newly founded nation. The Europeans viewed Franklin as a 'natural' genius.

I will return to the 'what if' view of my life later. For now, however, let us turn to the reality of my schooling.

Saint Francis Xavier Church
22 WEST HIGH ST. GETTYSBURG, PA

I had no idea how important a place St. Francis Xavier school and church would become to me. They dominated my life until I entered High School. As a student in the parish school and as an altar boy in the church, I learned the lessons that would guide me through life.

STARTING SCHOOL

In September of 1936, I was enrolled as a first grader at St. Francis Xavier Parochial School on High Street in Gettysburg. Today, the fees charged by private schools, religious or secular, would have prevented my family from enrolling me. In those days, there was no tuition charged at St. Francis. The monies to support the school came from a whole range of fund raising activities. (More about them later.)

A classmate of mine and a friend ever since, Marcus Steinour, recently reminded me that during recess on that first day, I slipped out. Apparently, with my schooling finished in less than a day, I'd run home. Marcus laughs when he describes seeing my Mother promptly dragging my reluctant body back. I suspect the Nuns labeled me as a troublemaker right then and there.

In the thirties, despite its German origins and Gettysburg's heavy percentage of German residents, there was no public kindergarten in Gettysburg. Curiously, this proved to be an advantage for me. My parents, with the help of relatives, had already started home schooling me.

My older cousin, Diddy, (Lillian Bowling) cut out the numbers and the letters of the alphabet and pasted them up on our kitchen walls. Every evening during the summer preceding my enrollment at St. Francis, my parents grilled me until I could recognize and say the alphabet as well as count. In short, I was given an advantage over the other beginning students. I could already recite the alphabet and count.

My first grade teacher was Sister Mary Damien. Sister Damien impressed me with two things, the need to be perfect in my studies and never to open my mouth or even twitch my lips until she called on me to recite. There were fifty, or more, students in Sister Damien's First and Second Grade Classes. She maintained order by outright intimidation. Her two primary teaching tools were the ruler and the yardstick. She employed both at the drop of a pencil and with incredible strength. She was fully dedicated to the wounding of young bare knuckles, butts and legs. Years later, Sister Damien and I were to agree that those measuring sticks were never used for measuring.

In the mid-90's, although now a Lutheran rather than a Catholic, I attended a fundraiser in Gettysburg for retired Nuns. As is well known, the Catholic Church had abdicated its responsibilities for many of the Sisters prior to that time. The question of what is owed to retired employees by any organization is an often debated one which deserves more attention. But that's not for discussion, not here and not at this moment. At the fundraiser, I said I felt all of my teachers at St. Francis were now deceased. To my great surprise, I was corrected. Sister Damien, now in her 90's, was much alive and living in a retirement home in Dallas, PA. My wife and I drove to Dallas to visit Sister Damien.

"Listen." I said to the Receptionist at the Nursing Home. "I want to have a spot of fun with Sister. Don't tell her my name. Just tell her I'm a former student." At that moment I had not seen Sister Damien for over fifty years. She had left Gettysburg in 1940.

"Well," replied the Receptionist. "I'll do it, but I don't think you can fool Sister. She's still very active. In fact, she's Chairman of the Craft's Section here."

In short order, a now tiny but spry old Nun appeared. I immediately pulled a paper from my pocket and waved it under her nose. "Sister Damien! I have a warrant for your arrest. The statute of limitations on child abuse never runs out and you've been accused of it by former students."

The statement startled her for just a second then she burst out in laughter in which I immediately joined.

"Sister." I asked seriously. "Do you remember how you used to beat my knuckles with a ruler? And how you used a little reed stick to hit me on the back of my legs? You realize that was for no reason at all. I was one of your best students."

"I don't know if I remember you or not. Help me a bit."

"I was an Altar Boy. I usually served the 5:30 Mass which you attended. I lived right around the corner from the Church. My Mother's name was Emma."

"Jakey Yingling!" After all those years, with just a touch of help, she'd recognized me instantly.

"Jakey, what have you been up to all this time?"

We sat down and I told her about my challenges, my exploits, some of my failures and some of my rewards.

"Well, well!" she said tartly. "I hope you know that any of those successes were because of what I taught you in the First and Second Grades."

At St. Frances Xavier Church, the teachers picked the Altar Boys. I was chosen in Second Grade. This was unusual because most boys were not selected until further along in the educational process. I was fortunate in that I had an excellent memory and could repeat back verbatim what the teacher told us during the class sessions. This was important because the Altar Boys had to learn the Latin Prayers and Responses used in the Mass. After all these years I can still repeat many of the prayers in Latin as well as most of the phrases used in response. I served as an Altar Boy from second grade through High School.

In 1938, when I was in Third Grade, my twin brother and Sister, Mark and Ave, were born. I remember they were born on a Saturday. My Father took me to his sister Marybelle's house while my Mother went to the Hospital. When he picked me up and told me the news, I became ecstatic. I was one of the few kids in the neighborhood who didn't have a brother or sister. And now, in one fell swoop, I had both.

In the Third Grade we were seated alphabetically so I sat in the last seat in the last row. Richard and Robert Riley sat right in front of me. That Sister had a hard time with me that day. I immediately, and incessantly, told Richard and Robert, as well as anyone else who would listen, about my new brother and sister.

With eight years difference between us, I became the twin's primary baby sitter and constant companion. That continued right up until they started First Grade and I moved into my first year at High School. The twins and I were very close during that time. I used to take them for their haircuts and, occasionally, we went to the movies together. This happened mostly when the theater had what they called a 'potato movie'.

We'd go down to the potato bin in the basement and put potatoes in a paper bar. This was the price of admission to the movie. The food collected on 'potato day' became the basis for food baskets which were distributed to area families on Thanksgiving and Christmas Day. We received two benefits from those potatoes. We saw the movies and we were one of the families on the list to receive a basket. That basket generally contained a chicken, canned foods and a stuffed toy. (Plus, of course, potatoes)

There were other support programs in the neighborhood. Many times, my Father and I walked down to the Firehouse together. I pulled a little wagon in which we carried home surplus foods such as flour, sugar, butter, and, infrequently, eggs. At Christmas time, the Firemen presented us with a box of candy and an orange. Christmas at home in those days was an excuse to give the children the inexpensive necessities of life such as stockings and underwear. We did not go overboard on items such as decorations or toys.

I had the same teacher in Grades Four, Five and Six and the routine continued. One of my primary memories of that time comes from joining up with Joe Cullison to go out collecting used newspapers. We took them to Morris Gittling's junkyard and sold them for a few cents. One day, with winter hard on us, we were collecting on Stevens street. I knocked on one door and a lady came out carrying a Mackinaw jacket instead of papers.

"Would you like to try this on?" she asked me. "If it fits you can keep it."

"Yes, Ma'am!" I replied instantly, hardly able to believe my luck.

All the way home from Stevens Street to Washington Street, I kept that jacket buttoned tight and my arms across it because Joe, who at that time was known as the toughest kid on the street, kept trying to take it off me. Needless to say, he didn't succeed. We'd agreed to go fifty-fifty on the papers, not on windfalls like this.

My weakest teacher at St. Francis taught Seventh Grade. She had trouble keeping order and never seemed quite prepared to teach. I spent a lot of time reading and learning on my own. Marcus Steinour confirms that he too read several books a week during that grade. In fact, when the teacher called on Marcus in class, he frequently was nose deep in a book and failed to respond. Marcus was one of the most intelligent kids in the class but she failed him. With deep regret, I moved on to eighth grade without him.

Those eight years at St. Francis set most of the parameters for my future life. I learned to manage detail. I learned to persist. I learned to work both hard and with intelligence. I learned that, although you can get help from outsiders, your best help always comes from family and from long time close friends. In short, the parochial education I received at St. Francis was a values oriented education.

That Church and that School were, for the most part, the centers of social activity, entertainment and cultural offerings within our neighborhood. As an example, in order to raise money for the School and the Parish, the Church held card parties each week. Five Hundred was the most popular card game at that time. Every Sunday the Priest announced ten names of people who were expected to provide prizes and food to be sold during the card games intermissions. The card games were well attended. Everybody in the neighborhood understood their importance. The card game revenue replaced tuition.

During those eight years at St. Francis there were two, so far not highlighted, factors which played a major role in my life: World War II and my Grandparents. In 1941 the Selective Service Act was passed and FDR was elected President for a Third Term. Churchill became the British Prime Minister. U.S. Savings Bonds and Stamps went on sale. Even I paused to read the newspapers with increased avidity. I realized that the blitzing of London by German bombers had brought war to an urban population in a way never before seen. To all of our friends who had registered for the draft, the threat of having to go into service had become very, very real. It was always a topic at the dinner table. **In fact, the possibility of our involvement in what would become World War II took over our lives.**

The bombing of Pearl Harbor by the Japanese added reality to the situation. It seemed me at that point that everybody had declared war on everybody else. All through 1943, I read about battle after battle in the papers I was delivering. In retrospect, what I did not read was that Hitler had begun murdering millions of Jews in gas chambers. Even now, I find the facts of that situation hard to comprehend.

In 1944 I moved on to the Ninth Grade and Gettysburg High School, a whole new educational experience.

MY INDOMITABLE GRANDPARENTS

By 1943 I had achieved a much deeper sense of family and of the role played in my life by my Grandparents. They were a major source of support during my growing up years. It was not so much a matter of physical or financial support as it was of knowing that they had survived lifetimes of crisis without losing their quite different senses of individuality. Some could talk with authority about their own family's involvement in wars stretching from the Revolutionary War to the Civil War to World War I. Others could detail changes in farming methods from decade to decade. They could all relate surprising facts about the changes which had occurred in Gettysburg during their life times.

On my Father's side, there were Matthew Matthias Yingling, known as 'Mac', and Lillian M. Weikert Yingling. On my Mother's side, there were Daniel Joseph Grimes and Harriet Bishop Grimes.

My Grandpa Yingling was born in Graceham, Maryland on February 11, 1870. He was baptized at St. Francis Anthony's Shrine Church in Emmitsburg, Maryland. His mother was Sarah Murray. She was the second wife of Jacob Yingling who had been born in 1815.

My Grandfather's Father had lived near Taneytown, MD. Several of his children were baptized at St. Joseph's Catholic Church in Taneytown. His first wife, Magdalene, is buried there in the Church Cemetery along with one of their infant children. After seven children, and the death of Magdalene, Jacob married Sarah Murray who had been born in France. Jacob and Sarah had four children, the last of whom was my Grandfather. He was the eleventh child sired by Jacob, whose name I bear.

Jacob married both wives at St. Joseph's. Sometime prior to 1870, Jacob moved to a farm located between Thurmont and Emmitsburg. My Grandfather, Matthew Matthias Yingling (Mac) was born in Graceham. Jacob Yingling died in 1892 at the age of 77. At the time, 'Mac' was 22. By my calculations, that means Jacob was 55 when he sired Mac.

In 1894, my Grandfather Mac, age 24, married Lillian M. Weikert of Gettysburg. The Weikerts were a prominent Gettysburg family while my Grandfather listed himself on the application as a 'laborer'. After their marriage, my Grandfather became a tenant farmer up until 1921. At that time he left farming and bought a house at 46 West Middle Street in Gettysburg. He stabled a team of horses and a wagon at the rear of his property and did hauling for a living. Later, he spent seven years working as a night watchman at the Gettysburg Furniture Factory.

Eventually, my Grandfather and Grandmother separated. They sold the Middle Street house and my Grandfather moved in with us at 229 South Washington Street in 1934. I have been told I shared a room with Grandpa, but I was only four and don't remember that. He stayed with us until 1937. At that time he voluntarily moved out to a room in the Monahan residence on Middle Street. He moved to make room for his oldest son, Clarence, my Father's brother and my uncle.

Clarence had just been released from prison in Philadelphia and the terms of his parole called for someone to be responsible for him. My Father assumed that role so Grandpa moved out and Clarence moved in. He stayed with us until 1938 when he had to move to make room for my new twin brother and sister.

Uncle Clarence never married. He was a big man but peaceful and caring. When just eleven or twelve, and playing in a baseball game, he'd been hit on the head with a bat. The injury necessitated placing a steel plate in his head. From time to time, the plate moved and caused him to become speechless and confused. This did not happen often but when it did happen at our house, I was the one who took him by the hand and led him out into the air. The fresh air seemed to help Clarence recover.

The fact that I, as a young boy, could take him outside to recover shows that there was no need to be frightened of him. However, later on he obtained a job at the Furniture Factory and underwent an attack while there. This led one of his co-workers to harass him. When Clarence grew tired of the taunting, he took up a knife and cut the shirt right off of the attacker. This was not done during his attack but immediately after he'd recovered. He was arrested and shipped off to prison in Philadelphia for one and a half years.

Clarence died in 1948 at the age of 53. He was a hard worker and had held a number of jobs, including working for the WPA with my Father in the stone quarry out on the Harrisburg Road. At that time, my Father was the first aid man at the site. I still have the manual studied by my Father in order to qualify for the position.

Grandma Yingling was the granddaughter of Jacob Weikert who owned the farm back of Big Round Top during the Battle of Gettysburg in 1863. Our first record of the Weikerts is with John Andrew Weikert who came over on the Neptune and arrived in Philadelphia on September 24, 1753. He and his son, Captain George Weikert, were both veterans of the Revolutionary War. George Weikert's father-in-law, Matthias Spitler, was also a veteran of the Revolutionary War. As research shows, I have many ancestors on both sides of the family who fought in that war.

Another Weikert of note was General John M. Weikert. He was born in 1898 and was a cousin of my Grandmother. He attended

Gettysburg High School and College and graduated from West Point in 1923. He was still living and active during World War II.

My Grandmother's father was David Weikert. He was the last child of Jacob Weikert and was fourteen years old during the Battle of Gettysburg. After the battle, he was helping clean the battlefield and managed to get blown up by the dynamite being used to remove the various shells and other ammunition. He was permanently blinded. In compensation, the Parks people permitted him to build a small store right across from Devil's Den. He ran that store for years.

David Weikert's sister, Henrietta, married George W. Shriver, who owned the Shriver House This has been restored and still stands as a tourist attraction. George W. Shriver enlisted in Cole's Calvary. He was ultimately captured and imprisoned in Andersonville. He died there, leaving Henrietta and the children to fend for themselves.

My Mother's parents were Daniel Joseph Grimes and Harriet Bishop. I have not yet succeeded in tracing the Grimes beyond my great Grandparents. 'Grimes' is a very common name in the Gettysburg area. I do know that my great grandfather Grimes, who lived in the Gettysburg area, later moved to Ohio or Indiana sometime prior to 1878. During this time my Grandfather Joseph Grimes was born there. Daniel Joseph Grimes and his wife Harriet had 14 children, one of whom died from eating bad oysters in 1917 and another who died during World War I of tuberculosis. This one was Retta, my Mother's older sister. Retta had been dating a soldier from Camp Colt known as 'Shorty' Burns. I was told Shorty came back to mourn her passing with my Grandparents. They evidently had been engaged.In 1926 when my Mother was sixteen, her parents lived in northern Adams County on a farm on Slaybaugh Road which was off the Carlisle Pike. My Grandfather moved to Carlisle to farm, then moved into Carlisle proper. He returned to the Gettysburg area in 1944 or 1945.

I was 14 or 15 at the time and had become increasingly aware that if the war continued, I would be called up. In 1944, American forces landed in Italy as well as on strange islands I had to look up in an Atlas. The coal mine strike came as a shock to me. I couldn't conceive of any union deliberately sabotaging the war effort. Things were dreadfully black and white for me during my high school days. In 1944 I cheered the landings in Normandy but was shocked when Count Ciano was reported to have been executed by his Father-in-law, Benito Mussolini. Then, FDR died and was succeeded by Harry Truman. Like most American GI's, I asked, "Harry who?"

A. Emma and her Sister Carrie.
B. Aunt Elsi, Aunt Carrie, Uncle Luther, Aunt Helen, and Emma.
C. Emma with her Grandsons and their children.

Matthew Matthias Yingling
Lillie May Weikert Yingling
Jacob Charles Yingling
Norman Yingling
Maybelle Yingling
Clarence Yingling
My Dad has his hand on his Father's knee.

MY MOTHER, THE SURVIVOR

My Dad and Mother were married in April of 1926. My Mother was just sixteen, 'young but mature' I've been told. The economy was still booming. There was no reason for them to suspect the chaotic financial conditions that would prevail after the stock market crash of 1929. It had been nearly fifty years since the country had undergone a serious depression (1873) and no one remembered how bad that had been. My Mother spoke to me about this many years after I'd graduated from college.

"You have to understand what life was like in a small town in those days. There wasn't too much recreation for young people. Men worked long days and saving money wasn't all that easy. As a result, men married later and girls married younger. Just like your Dad and I did." Mom never felt she'd been singled out by the fickle finger of fate. After all, most of the women she knew were in the same sinking boat.

My Father and Mother met at a barn dance. According to what I have been told about those early barn dances, there was always someone there with a fiddle. There was a beatable washtub and a harmonica or two. The dance took place in a real working barn. There was hay and probably a syncopated horse or cow looking on from its stall. The working barn had a central space cleared for the dancers. The non-dancers stood around and clapped time with their hands. "And let the Ho-down begin!" One stroke of the bow across the fiddle strings and away the dancers went, not to stop till the fiddle player collapsed. "Let's change partners with a do-see-do!" And, once again, away they'd go.

The courtship didn't move all that fast. Dad met Mom when she was just 15. He'd come by to see her every once and a while up till they married. But that took a while. She was almost 17 when they stood up in the Rectory at St. Francis Xavier in Gettysburg and declared their vows. Seventeen months later, in September 1927, Mom gave birth to my sister, Joanna. She only lived seventeen months. My little sister died due to what might be called malpractice today. The Doctors gave her a shot for diphtheria. Later, it was determined that she'd had complications resulting from the measles.

I have a picture of my Mom when she was twelve or fourteen years old. When it was taken, she had been out working for nearly three years. She'd had to leave school in the third grade to help support the family. At ten years of age she'd hired out for a dollar and a quarter a week. This is why I am indeed sure she was much more mature at age sixteen than you might reasonably have expected. Necessity and work almost always bring unanticipated maturity too quickly to young children.

My Mother was an older child in a very large family. Her father was a tenant farmer and not thriving, not even in what seemed, at that time, to be a thriving economy. Of course, we have all learned the hard way that the bottom of the economic barrel seldom benefits, not even by a hurricane of prosperity topside. In those days, my Mother would leave early in the morning and come home late in the evening. Her dollar and a quarter a week went to her parents, not to her. On another job she left home on Monday and returned on Friday evening. For the same dollar and a quarter a week, she milked cows. Another time, she worked a team of horses pulling a plow.

Her brother, Jacob, had died in 1917 from eating bad oysters, or so she'd been told. Her older sister, Mary, left home at age 15 to marry. With Mary's departure, it was my Mother's turn to leave the home and go to work. It wasn't that her parents didn't love her. It was the pure and evil economics of family survival on a hardscrabble farm.

"I had to milk the cows. I had to clean the house. I had to be a servant even when one old Lady was so mean to me I wanted to spit in her face.. All of this for a dollar and a quarter a week."

Marriage didn't change things much for Mom. To help out in their early struggle, Mom used to do what we called 'day work'. She went out and cleaned people's houses. Even when my Dad was on the WPA and getting a regular salary, she cleaned people's houses. She took care of everything from scrubbing the commodes to making their beds. Mom did whatever had to be done. She did that even after the twins, Mark and Ave, were born.

Up until World War II started, my Mother did her wash by hand. She heated water in a big wash boiler, put in the clothes and stirred them with a paddle. Then, she rinsed them, wrung them out by hand, and hung them out on lines. With Dad making more money during the war economy, he bought her a washing machine. Then, she started taking in other people's laundry.

As I remember, she did about ten washes a week for other people. This included both washing and ironing. It was hard, hard work. It was almost slave labor. I remember that Dad was able to buy her the washer with a wringer, but not a clothes dryer. Everything was hung on the line. Then, it had to be taken down and re-dampened for ironing.

Mom did laundry for people such as Dr. Kramer at the College; Admissions Dean Hipps Wolf, and Mrs. Topper. She was the wife of a local attornry. I remember Mr. and Mrs. Foth especially because they lived on the third floor of what was then the First National Bank Building.

That was in downtown Gettysburg on the Square. I remember them because I was the one who picked up and delivered their laundry. I was the one who climbed those three flights of stairs twice each week.

I also especially remember Dr. Kramer. It was over a mile out to his house. I was about eleven at the time and I always, even in the rain, pulled my wagon out to pick up their wash. It was a complete wash, not just bed sheets like Mom did for some people. It was always a heavy load. Worse yet, I had to pull it all the way back through town. I always did it, but I also hoped I would not see any of my friends from school while I was doing it. A lot of Mom's regular customers were the parents of friends of mine from school. I know now it was stupid of me to feel embarrassment. But at the time I was just a kid. I did feel embarrassed.

My Mother also cleaned Dr. Knox's office. He had been a surgeon in the army but received a discharge before the war ended. When he opened his office in Gettysburg, Mom contracted to clean it every Friday night. I helped her scrub and wax the floors. Sometimes, she gave me a quarter for doing this. I think she was only getting a quarter an hour herself so that quarter was a significant part of her pay.

I realize now that Mom was respected by the affluent people around town for whom she worked. They accepted her for the trustworthy and pleasant person that she was. And she earned enough money to help my Dad pull together the funds needed to buy a house in 1951.

Mom was a hard worker. She wasn't arrogant, but she never seemed to feel inferior. No matter who she talked to or who she worked for, she held her own. She was never afraid to stand on her own dignity.

I had special relationships with both my Mother and my Father. I had bonded very early with my Father as a result of spending every hour of every day with him when I was very young.. On the other hand, I don't recall my Father ever kissing me. I remember my Mother doing this. Even when I was the ripe old age of eight or nine, she still occasionally pulled me onto her lap to hold and rock me.

One other thing I need to say about my Father. Even though both my parents realized they would never be able to pay my way through college, my Dad, even when I was just a young child, said "Jakey, you should plan to go to college."

I know now that my Dad saw that successful people went to college. They got an education. To my Dad, an education guaranteed success. He made sure I understood just exactly how important a college education could be. Unlike a lot of my friends who had no hope of ever going on in education, I always understood that getting good grades was important. So I did. I pulled good grades even when I had no idea of how I could ever pay for a college education.

Of course, every day I realize more and more that my parents were unlettered but not uneducated. They kept up with the times. They read newspapers and scanned the magazines which Mom sometimes picked from the throw away pile at the homes and offices she cleaned. Their advise to me was frequently couched with quotes about the news. They stayed abreast of what they saw as important trends: the forming of the United Nations, Truman's creation of the Atomic Energy Commission, the first verdicts handed down in the Nuremberg Trials. Mom was fascinated by Princess Elizabeth's marriage to Lord Philip Mountbatten, Duke of Edinboro while Dad deplored enactment of the Taft Hartley Act restricting Labor Unions

Mom and Dad.

SHE ALREADY KNEW

It was my ardent wish that this book would be finished in time for my Mother to hear certain passages from it. Many of the good things which happened in my life came as a direct result of her intervention: growing up in Church, transferring to Gettysburg College from East Stroudsburg, acceptance of my early marriage within the family, indeed, development of my entire ethical make-up was because I always felt her presence during critical decisions.

But it was not meant to be. My Mother passed away on November 17, 1999. This was just about one month before her ninetieth birthday. Her death came as a massive shock to me. The doctors had decided that she needed a cardiac pacemaker to help her failing circulation. The day before the scheduled operation I spent most of the day just sitting and chatting with her. The next morning she was prepped for the surgery, then, while on the table waiting, my Mother suffered a major and overwhelming heart attack.

My first word of her death came when a nurse approached me and told me the Doctor wished to speak with me in the Hospital Chapel. At the time I did not understand the significance of her request. There was that moment of stunned silence on my part, then I was overwhelmed by a deep, deep sense of loss. I felt a loss I could only express with sobs and tears. Thank God, I was immediately surrounded by family. They shared my grief and helped me move through the necessities of the next few days. For the first time I think I understood the pain suffered by those who must bear such grief alone.

A close friend of mine wrote me a note saying he was sorry my Mother didn't get to read about the special relationship we shared and how deep my love for her was. But I truly have no regrets about that. I often told my Mother how I loved her and we'd often relived in conversation the incidents referred to in this book.

We often talked about the sacrifices she had made for me and the wonderful moments we'd shared. We often gossiped about the old days and the characters we'd known. My Mom didn't have to read these pages to know how I felt about her. She already knew! But, still and all, the loss was overwhelming. Perhaps the following poem will help explain my feelings. I copied it from a sheet of Avis letterhead I found in the Albuquerque Airport.

Why I Cry

The emptiness
  At being
    Left behind.
The memory
  Of your hand
    Holding mine.
A smile
  That made the
    World seem bright.
Laughter
  Like music
    Filling the night.
The words
  That said how
    Much we cared.
The happiness
  That we both shared
Is why
  I cry
    Since you're gone.

Although most of my family had turned away from the Catholic Church, Momma had not. She was born a Lutheran but became a Catholic at age 16 when she married my Father. She remained a devoted Catholic all her life and she died with in the arms of the Catholic Church.

In a sense my Mother's funeral service carried me back to my own church roots. Thanks to Momma, I grew up a member of St. Francis Xavier Parish in Gettysburg. Before 1831 Catholics living in Gettysburg attended mass in Conewago. By wagon or by foot this was seven hours each way. Occasionally, the Jesuits reversed the trip to conduct services in a private residence in Gettysburg.

On October 3, 1831 a new church was dedicated at a site one and one half blocks southwest of the current site. Its first Pastor was Father Michael Dougherty, a Jesuit from Conewago and a native of Ireland. The early parishioners were mostly German immigrants and the congregation sang hymns in the German language until 1843.

The current church was dedicated on July 31, 1853 by the priest who was to become known as Saint John Neumann. Ten years later the church served as a hospital during the Civil War. Care of the wounded fell to the Sisters of Charity from Emmitsburg. On hearing of the battle they had quickly journeyed to Gettysburg in two carriages. The Church continued as a hospital for two months after the battle. It then remained closed for repairs until January of 1864.

After the Civil War the Parish opened its own school. By 1896 there were 128 students sharing one room with three classes taking place at the same time. It cost fifty cents a month to attend. During World War I the Parish once again operated an army hospital to care for the soldiers from nearby Camp Colt. Over five thousand of them contracted the flu during the epidemic of 1918.

In 1920 the Sisters of Charity ended their long years of dedication to the Parish School. The Pastor at that time, Father Boyle, invited the Sisters of Mercy to staff the school. Sister Mary Angela, accompanied by four other sisters, arrived in Gettysburg in August of 1920. The Sisters of Mercy continued to serve as teachers on beyond the time when I was a student in the Parish School. A new school was constructed in 1950 and the Church itself underwent construction in 1953, in time for the 100th anniversary of its founding.

Beyond attending the Parish School, I was selected to serve as an Altar Boy in the Church. During my years as an Altar Boy. the Mass was still presented in Latin. Even today, I can still recite faithfully and truly all of the invitations and responses to the Mass as they were presented then.

I have detailed my growing up within the Catholic Church because I found my Mother's funeral to be so moving an experience that it carried me nearly back to my very roots. Whatever quarrel I may have within myself concerning the Catholic Church, my protest is at the actions of the hierarchy, even at items such as the recent pronouncement that Martin Luther had not really erred sufficiently to justify his excommunication. My quarrel has never been with the good people within the Parish, not even though my good friend Marcus Steinour and I still carp about raps on the knuckles and switch marks on the legs delivered by overly zealous Nuns at school.

I was so moved by the service that after the communion mass was nearly over, I arose and approached the Priest to ask that I be served communion. I understood full well that this was not in accordance with church protocol but I felt deeply moved to do it. I knew my Mother would applaud one more act of rebellion on my part since it was in her memory and to her honor. The Priest instantly acceded. I'm sure he understood my motives.

"What else is there to say, Momma? My grief will continue until we meet again. Your life was truly an act of AMAZING GRACE and your memory will linger on far beyond the day of your passing."

A. Marianne, Emma, and Cindi.
B. Randy, Emma, and Steve.

WHAT IF THE DICE HAD ROLLED DIFFERENTLY

The first conclusion about my life must be that, even had I existed as a European, probably as a German, my life never could have traveled the course it did. I would have come of age in Hitler's Germany. I would have been subjected to all the cruelties of the time. I would have had none of the opportunities I discovered in the United States. Possibly, I might have been named 'Juengling', been a Lutheran, perhaps even a post World War II government official, or even a banker. But I fear not!

I'm of a disposition to feel that at my age in the Forties there would have been little choice but to become a member of the Hitler Youth Movement. If I had been extraordinarily lucky, I would have been drafted into a military unit which was captured by the Americans and sent to a stateside prisoner of war camp, maybe even to one my home town, Westminster, MD.

I, too, could have worked with the local farmers and ended up friends with many Americans. The men I know of in Germany to whom this happened still feel pleased at having lost their battle and being carried off to safety, to live and not fight another day. Two of them worked for Carroll County farmer Roger Roop and his wife, Olive. They ate well and were only attacked on occasion by morons from the local ultra-nationalistic right. These attackers, incidentally, were in all probability also of German descent but had forgotten their own roots.

Of course, in my case, I doubt I would have been so lucky. I would have been seen as cannon fodder and I doubt that I would have survived the war. I never would have had a career, nor married, nor had children.

Christian Juengling's desire for a better life and his decision to follow William Penn's siren call was the first step in my becoming the person I became. I inherited Christian's DNA but without the burden of German history or the unfortunately limited prospects which existed for a German youth of my age and status after World War II.

I Was Extraordinarily Fortunate To Have Chosen My Parents So Wisely.

This is my second major conclusion. I can't believe that anyone could have read this far in the book without recognizing the debt I owe to both my parents. My Mother was what I have termed 'A Survivor'. My Father is deserving of the same descriptor. Both or them did whatever it took, not just to stay alive but to grow personally and to help their children grow in every way possible. They didn't always agree about what was best for me, but each of them gave me every boost they could. It was important to them that their children go further than their limited opportunities had permitted them to go.

The Impact of the Stock Market Crash and the Depression On My Life.

(What conclusion do you suggest I should draw about the world going to hell in a hand basket just one year before I was born?)

First, let me mention the best thing that could have come out of such a bad situation. Earlier, I mentioned the obscene unemployment situation created by the economic folly wrought by the so-called financial literati of the world. Note the word 'world'! The United States was not in the soup bowl alone. The entire world was in there with us.

The **good thing** was that my Father never could have spent the time he did with me if he'd had to go to work every day. Those were hard and cruel times for my parents. In fact, the threat of starvation hung heavy over the heads of some of our family members. This ' unemployed' time permitted my Father and me to bond in a way which could not have occurred under any other circumstance. As it was, we spent all day, everyday, together. We came to know and understand each other as only constant companions can.

At that time I was far too young and uneducated to even have an opinion as to how to solve the problems caused by the Crash and the Depression. When I did encounter the twin questions of causation and cure, first in High School, then in College, I was given information which has, of late, proved to be, at the very least, suspect.

In the broadest terms, I was told that the Stock Market Crash was due to investors buying too heavily on margin. No blame was assigned to the sellers or enablers of the process. The teachers claimed that the Depression was caused by the Stock Market Crash. World War II put people back to work and cured the Depression's primary component, **unemployment.** How is that for over-simplification of a truly complex puzzle?

[Henry Ford's analysis of the unemployment situation in 1931 was a typical masterpiece of entrepreneurial idiocy and managerial malpractice. He said: in March, the crisis is here because "the average man won't really do a full day's work unless he is caught and can't get out of it. There is plenty of work to do if people would do it." Howard Zinn in his book on The Twentieth Century reports next that: **'A few weeks later he laid off 75,000 workers."** Take your choice. Was it hypocrisy or stupidity?]

As I see it, today the ultimate cause of the Depression is now recognized by most economists to lie in the First World War and the collapse of what was known as the Industrial Revolution. In the Thirties, the advent of the Technological Revolution led to over production which went unrecognized. Recognition came only after World War II and full development of new Technologies has not yet peaked.

In summary, between 1920 and 1930, economists had to stop worrying about America's productive capabilities and turn to questioning America's capacities to consume. (It is increasingly obvious that we now know that America will never be able to consume everything it can produce, nor can it produce everything we wish to manufacture at competitive prices for the world market we'd like to own. That's a topic for another ten or twenty books, most of them to follow whatever the next economic crisis may prove to be. I make no pretense of being a futurist so I'll leave that to the same people who are forecasting a doubling of our population by 2100.)

In support of this theory of causation consider the following. During the Industrial Revolution, productivity went up 43% while factory worker's wages increased only 20%. At the same time industrial profits were put into dividends, more machines or outright speculation in other ventures. They did not go to the people who would use the money to buy the items they produced.

The monetary values held by private individuals nose dived as industry after industry fell into the hands of monopolies. For example, by 1930 one-half of the electrical output in the United States was controlled by three enormous holding companies. One half of the non-banking corporate wealth was held by the 200 largest corporations. These, in turn, were owned by some 2,000 individual executives and financiers.

Top this off by having the farm sector collapse. Farm bankruptcies multiplied six times over to the point where, in the late Twenties, farmers were leaving the farms at a rate of 600,000 per year. They crowded into the cities to help create the specter of unemployment with which FDR was faced. You should note that most farmers could not sell their farms at any price. They just fled and left their unpaid mortgages behind.

I am almost overwhelmed by a sense of déjà vu as I write these words. It is like watching an early black and white motion picture about the movements of my own family. The only good thing I can point out is that, so long as our roots were on the farm (as were my wife's completely) we didn't starve. Even if the family could not sell the food they grew, they could eat it.. IF ONLY THE BANKERS DID NOT FORECLOSE ON THE MORTGAGE!

In summary, the roots of the Depression were growing long before the Stock Market crashed. The effects of the crash were to administer the coup de grace to the economy and throw the impact of monopolistic practices and poor government policy back into the faces of the people who had created the situation. In short, the nation and the world harvested the fruits of unchecked greed. Unfortunately, but only in retrospect, we now recognize that the Crash itself was forecast by the Credit Mobiler scandal of the 1800's and the panic of 1907.

It is absolutely true that the Crash was at least partly caused by the practice of brokers selling 'on margin' .A customer could put down ten or twenty percent on a block of stock and the broker essentially loaned the missing monies. When things began to go badly, the customers did not have the cash to make up the difference. Mostly, they lost everything.

Accompanying the margin catastrophe was the formation of 'investment trusts'. They offered an opportunity for the small investor to get heavily into the 'bull' market prevailing at that time. Unfortunately, the investment trusts were mostly unregulated. Many of the 500 trusts existing in 1929 had put their money primarily into other investment trusts. This created a house of cards which collapsed.

People like Andrew Mellon, then Secretary of the Treasury, and President Hoover recognized the danger but could not bring themselves to interrupt a situation by which both had profited handsomely. The sheer volume of trading should have warned them to take action.

During the critical years of 1926 to 1929, trading had risen from 451 million shares to over 1.1 billion shares. Many government officials had participated in the 250% growth in paper profits. They, too, had bought low (some on the basis of insider information) and sold high.

The hour by hour details of the Crash, which began on September 3, 1929 and climaxed on October 29, 1929, read like a novel. In this context it is important to note that the bankers failed the country. They could not come to the market's rescue. Instead, the Bankers, themselves, were hiding in their offices, paralyzed by fear.

It was as though the ghost of Lenin had reached out from Russia and seized the Bankers by their gonads as he had the economists of Russia some ten years before.

What this all meant to me was that I was to grow up in a world of unemployed men, unstable finances and political pontificating by uneducated politicians who demonstrated little understanding of the actual causes of the nation's poverty. This had a reverse effect on me because, early on, I saw the need to build a backlog of money – thus my fixation on banks, bankers and banking. I knew from age five that I needed an income and took steps to procure one. Beyond that I also discovered that whatever came to me must be inspired by my own internal desire. And my own desires were not spelled out primarily in terms of owning 'things' but in terms of my own willingness to work hard, intelligently and in the light of my need to secure my own future.

Now, let me return briefly to what my future might have been had my family never left Germany. Only lately have I begun to understand the effects of 'our' Depression and the Stock Market crash on other countries. Surprisingly, I've discovered that many people believe that the Crash had a far greater impact on Germany than anywhere else, even including the United States.

The Crash caused American banks to refuse to renew many short-term loans to Germany. If this is a topic of interest to you, please read The Great Depression by John A. Garraty. He spells out beautifully the impact this withholding of funds had on international politics and the economic forces which led Hindenberg to appoint Hitler Chancellor. To me, it seems evident that Hitler could not have been appointed had the American banks been able to continue their loans to Germany.

Back in the United States, the inadequacies of Coolidge and Hoover when coupled with their adherence to the desires of their patrician friends were corrected by the greatest patrician of them all, FDR. He still goes down in my history book as the greatest friend the common man ever had. In my case, had he done nothing else, the creation of the WPA would have proved to be the start of our family's recovery from poverty. I still applaud that and deny that anyone other than FDR (including Einstein) should have been appointed 'the greatest man of the century".

(According to Joseph Lash in his book Dealers and Dreamers, Roosevelt had picked up the theme of 'The Forgotten Man' from Raymond Moley. Moley explained to his sister that Roosevelt "was trying to reach the underdog and I scraped from my memory an old phrase "The Forgotten Man' which had haunted me for years." Al Smith, already a candidate, had a hizzy fit over Roosevelt's use of the term. Smith regarded himself as the champion of the masses. This became the issue of issues in the 1932 campaign and probably, according to Judge Brandeis, handed Roosevelt the election.

I have now spoken of the exodus of my family from Germany (from the Palatine in all probability), the influence of my parents, and the impact of the Stock Market Crash as well as a slight mention of the Depression Years. Now, it is time to return to my growing up years, to the family and to the community.

A. Jake alone.
B. Jake with his teammates: Bob Foth, Tom Hemingway, Bob Shetter, Jake, Bill Shaw.

ON TO HIGH SCHOOL

There was a Catholic High School, Delone, located in McSherrytown, but, at that time, there were no buses available to make the run from Gettysburg. Therefore, the kids who graduated from St. Francis mostly transferred to the public high school, in Gettysburg. There are three things I need to say about my time at Gettysburg High School.

First of all, physically I grew like the proverbial bad weed. I was on the small side when I enrolled in ninth grade, but, by the time I became a junior, I'd reached six feet and was big enough to play high school football successfully.

Second, I became gainfully employed, and while still keeping my studies in good order, saved enough money to make the possibility of going to college seem real.

One of my most productive jobs was at the A&P store in Gettysburg. I worked there after football season in my junior year. Two of my classmates, Jim Slaybaugh and Don Hoff, worked in the meat department. Galen Keeney, who later became a physician, was a stock clerk. I became a cashier because I was very good at moving the groceries with one hand and making entries on the keyboard at the same time with the other. Don't scoff. It's the little things which lead to success in life. In this case it was timing. In the modern store with its moving counter, I'd have possessed no edge.

In this same vein, while going to college in those days was an order of magnitudes less costly than today, I was still dreadfully naïve about the real costs of living away from home and paying the minimal bills I'd incur.

My third comment about my High School Days is that this is where I discovered that girls were different and Vive La Difference and all that. In truth, most importantly, I met the girl I'd ultimately marry and we gradually bonded. Naturally, that path was not without some twists, turns, bumps and occasional disjunctions. Is it ever?

MEETING GENNY

My future wife, Genevieve Koontz, was born on a farm near Gettysburg. Genny attended a one room schoolhouse through sixth grade. Then, her parents moved into Gettysburg and she enrolled in the public school system. By 1944, she was a freshman at Gettysburg High School along with me and one hundred fifty other kids.

We didn't meet in our freshman or sophomore classes. I was in the academic program and she'd enrolled in the commercial program. We had no classes together and I can't even remember passing her in the halls. I did see Genny in my junior year since she was an excellent dancer and active in the Girls Athletic Association.

In my senior year, on home football game days, almost the entire school attended a pep rally in the auditorium or gym. Senior girls who were members of the Athletic Association wore the football player's jerseys. The girl I was dating at the time wasn't a senior so she couldn't wear my jersey. When the girls came out at the pep rally, there was Genny wearing my jersey.

"What's Koontz doing with my jersey?" I asked a friend.

Only later did I find out that Genny had wrestled it away from another girl so she could wear it. I took a good look at 'the Koontz girl' that day! Genny Koontz was pretty and she had a really nice pair of legs. That was the first time I took special notice of Genevieve Koontz.

Important things never move in a straight line for me, so it was months later before I once again encountered Genny. This time I was in a school play and Genny was a member of the make-up crew. She volunteered to help with my make-up. A few nights later, the play committee decided to go out for a coke and hamburger. I said I couldn't go because my steady girlfriend was waiting outside for me.

"No problem!" said one of Genny's chums. "I'll go out and tell her there's going to be extra practices and she might as well go home." With that Genny took my hand.

"Let me show you how to get out the back door." she said. I was out that door and on my way for a coke and hamburger before I could think about saying 'no'.

Several weeks later, the senior class went to Washington on a class trip. I was late getting on the bus. All of the seats, except one, had been taken. Genny had kept the one next to her open. For almost three days, we spent a lot of time getting to know each other really well.

But again, my life never seems to move in straight lines. I didn't follow up. In fact, I think I danced with Genny just once after that. It was at a school dance which came late in my senior year. Right after graduation, I spent my days working in the Poconos. This was to fill in some time and to accumulate more money before I left for college. The day before I was to leave for the Poconos, I spent the day up at Marsh Creek Heights where my girlfriend's parents owned a small store and cabin. She stayed on there while I caught a ride back to Gettysburg so I could catch a bus to the Poconos the next day. Almost on a whim, I called Genny that evening.

"Hey, Gen." I said. "We haven't seen each other since graduation. How are you doing?"

"Why don't you come on out to the house and we can talk about a lot of things. " I thought that, despite the way I'd ignored her, Genny sounded downright friendly.

We did, indeed, cover a lot of ground. We covered so much that, at the end of the evening, Genny asked if she could write to me while I was away. During that summer and all through that first year in college, I received many letters from Genny, all of which I still have.

Genny had gone to work for the telephone company and found a reason to call me at least once a week while I was away at college. I've never been sure exactly how long it took me to unwarp my thinking and for Genny and me to become steadies. But it did happen. As fate would have it, the unwarping of my emotional confusion was the best thing that ever happened to me.

I realize now that completing High School and starting College became so totally self-absorbing that I almost totally disengaged from both my family and from the world outside my own immediate concerns. Events which would have totally bemused me, such as Truman's reelection, the establishment of the Israeli State, the conviction of Alger Hiss on perjury charges and Joe McCarthy's claim that the government was totally riddled with communists eluded my consciousness.

EAST STROUDSBURG STATE COLLEGE

During my last spring semester at Gettysburg High School, I took a bus up to East Stroudsburg State College for an interview. My parents had to work and were not able to go with me. This blew the primary interviewer's mind.

"It's most unusual, Jake." said the clerk in the Assistant Dean's office. "As a matter of fact, it's unheard of for a seventeen year old boy to be interviewed without his parents."

"I'm sorry." I replied quietly, not at all sure the interview was going to proceed if I didn't suddenly produce my parents. "But it can't be helped. They're working. They can't afford to take a day off to help me with something they feel I can handle on my own."

Things were still very tight for our family in 1947. I didn't tell any of the interviewers just how tough conditions really were. But, in fact, they were so tough that, since it was still frigid outside, I had to borrow a top coat from a cousin just to make the trip to Stroudsburg without looking ridiculous. I owned a jacket and an old sport coat, but, even to me, they seemed too old and too shabby to support the responsible image I hoped to present. As it was, the interviewers still cut immediately to the core of the problem.

"Tell me, Mr. Yingling, exactly how is your education going to be financed?

"Well, that's not all settled but I have saved a thousand dollars so far. I earned that money shoveling snow, working a paper route, and I've been tending furnaces in the neighborhood since I was ten. I clerked in a grocery store for the past three years and I'll be working in the Poconos this next summer."

I didn't tell those people in the Admissions Office that I'd decided I would never let a ten year old boy, even a supposedly intelligent and responsible one, take care of my furnace if I ever owned a house. Fortunately, they didn't ask that kind of question and I slid through the interview OK. I got out of there just as soon as they allowed as how they'd accept me. I was smart enough to not want to hear the odds they'd place on my actually finding enough money to make it through college.

As you can guess, I'd bitten off more than I could chew. That Freshman Year, 1948-49 was to become my year in purgatory. As a good Catholic, I never quite slipped into Hell, but I came close enough to be sure Dante never actually visited that real hot spot. If he'd experienced the purgatorial depths into which I'd fallen, the poetry would have been crisped right out of his body. Beatrice would have been nothing but a faint, if erotic, memory. Dante never would have finished his books., not even Il Paradiso.

Part of my problem came from not wanting to admit to my three roommates how limited my funds were or how frugal I had to be. They were all relatively affluent. One was a veteran attending college on the GI Bill. One fellow's father had a supervisory sales job and the third came from a family which kept him fully funded.

My roommates never intended to be cruel to me, but I just couldn't' admit the state of my personal finances to them. As an example, I only had one pair of leather shoes and one pair of gym shoes. Neither was expensive and both were so worn that I had fitted them with cardboard inserts. When you wear the same shoes all the time, eventually they stink. Mine became downright disagreeable.

"Why don't you deep six those gadamn things and get some decent shoes?"

I didn't even answer. Money was so tight I couldn't buy another pair no matter how offensive they'd become. If I bought new shoes I'd have to give up eating that week. As it was I ate at the lowest possible subsistence level. I tried to convince myself I was just being frugal and not really starving.. The second semester I stopped eating in the dining room at all. I'd finally realized I just couldn't afford it.

There was a small diner in East Stroudsburg where, for five dollars, you could buy a five dollar and fifty cent meal ticket. And, believe it or not, I would try to stretch that five dollar and fifty cent meal ticket over two weeks. By the end of the second week, my meal ticket would have expired and I'd not eat from Thursday until I'd hitchhiked home on Friday and could sit down at the family table.

My Mother was concerned about me hitchhiking back and forth from East Stroudsburg. I made the trip as often as I could. Sometimes, I left at 4 o'clock Friday afternoon when my class ended and made it to Gettysburg by midnight. I was almost always lucky enough to get fast rides. People were still willing to pick up young people on the move as they had all through World War II. I usually covered the one hundred and sixty miles in seven or eight hours.

When coming home, I always brought along my dirty clothes. I never told my Mother I was hungry, but if there was fruit or a can of anything, I'd ask:

"Mom, what are you doing with that?"

"Nothing." She'd reply.

"Well then, can I have it?"

Sometimes I was able to carry a can of pork and beans back to school with me. I'd open the can and eat them cold after my roommates had departed for the cafeteria. I know my Mother suspected what I was doing, but she never asked a question since we both knew there was no answer.

My Dad sometimes offered me five dollars to buy a bus ticket back to Stroudsburg. In 1948 things had become just a bit better for my parents. But I always tried to save the five dollars anyway. Instead of taking the bus, I'd hitchhike to Harrisburg. If I arrived there in time, I would try to catch the bus to Easton. If I missed it, as I mostly did, I'd hitchhike to Easton. If I arrived in Easton in time, I'd try to take the last bus to Stroudsburg. If I missed that, as I mostly did, I wouldn't get back to my room until one o'clock Sunday morning.

My Mother was aware of all this although I never brought it up. One day she asked me quietly: "Jakey, why don't you go to school in Gettysburg?"

The original decision to go to East Stroudsburg State College had been heavily influenced by a guidance counselor at Gettysburg High. She knew I wanted to be a teacher and a football coach. She'd suggested Stroudsburg because it was well known for its teaching program and for its football team as well. This was why I originally applied there. But neither my family nor I had known it would prove to be quite so hard to manage. My Mother persisted.

"Jakey, why don't you go to Gettysburg?"

"I don't know, Mom. I really don't know."

"Jakey, would you mind if I see what I can do for you?"

My Mother was a woman with a third grade education but a woman with style, a woman who felt comfortable with all kinds of people. Emma Yingling was a woman who was well-respected for herself. She also was a woman who felt confident enough within herself to approach the right people with her problem.

The right people in this case were two high placed staff members at Gettysburg College. These were people for whom she did laundry. One was Doctor Kramer, head of the Education Department. The other was Hipps Wolf, Dean of Admissions. She simply called up Dean Wolf and said: "I want Jakey to go to Gettysburg College."

"Is he a good student?" Dean Wolf never asked my Mother about money. He knew my parents were very poor.

"Naturally, he's a good student." Replied my Mother. "Jakey's always been a good student."

"Alright, Mrs. Yingling. Have his transcripts sent to me at the College."

And that was a done deal. On receiving my transcripts, they decided I was admissible and sent me a letter so stating.. There is no question. My Mother was solely responsible for getting me transferred to Gettysburg. She'd had the courage to take the bull by the horns. She'd called Dean Wolf and told him she wanted her son transferred to Gettysburg and he'd seen her request as real, honest and deserving. To me, it seemed like a miraculous intervention. I'd been handed a ticket out of the purgatory into which I'd wandered so inadvertently. Getting back to Gettysburg removed the pain.

GOING HOME TO GETTYSBURG

Over a lifetime, I've returned to Gettysburg many times from many places. Each time it's a new homecoming. I live again the memories of my family, the foods we enjoyed, the fields we ran in as children, and even the ghosts which persistently haunt the town. Don't scoff. Only a deeply-rooted-in-history town has ghosts. Now, when I walk about the streets I trod as a boy, I don't just see what currently exists. I see old friends, mourn long destroyed buildings, recall conversations held years before, some with people who've been dead for more years than I care to detail.

This first homecoming, in many ways, was a shock to me. I hadn't been gone that long but I doubted I'd ever return to my own reality. I didn't feel the homecoming, I'm sure, with all the pulse pounding thrill of a veteran who'd made it through the war alive, but I did feel the same overwhelming sense of being back in my own time and my own place. That's the guts of déjà vu isn't it? The recognition of a world you may have felt you'd lost, never to be regained.

For example, let's talk about food. When you don't have ample food, you develop vivid memories of what good food you did have when you had it. In Stroudsburg State College I'd often thought of Gettysburg two major bakeries: Henning's Bakery on York Street and The Model Steam Bakery. In those days their trucks toured our neighborhood. Other people bought from the trucks but we didn't. My Mother baked a lot because flour and sugar were cheap. Sometimes, not often, she made buns, big butterfly buns. I only got to eat them on rare occasions but I've never forgotten how big they were or their sweet delicate taste.

I had a paper route which let me work my way past another bakery, Reuning's on Baltimore Street. I'd stop in there and ask if they had any day-old buns. These sold for a penny a piece. I'd try to get there in time to buy two pennies worth. Since I was always late, I didn't succeed too often, but when I did, those buns were a mouth watering treat.

Along with buns, we kids had a fixation on strawberries. About the time the twins were born in the Thirties, we used to hike out a path which ran along Long Lane. This was the path followed by the CCC men when they came in from West Confederate Avenue. It led them right past Breckenridge Street where the black girls lived. At the end of Long Lane there was a field of wild strawberries. We picked these in season and my Mother made strawberry jam. Unfortunately, that field is now covered with houses.

Also, at the place where the railroad tracks crossed Long Lane, there was a big hickory nut tree. My Dad always tried to get there at the time the hickory nuts fell. We'd gather up what we could find. Then, at Christmas, my Mother would bake a hickory nut cake.

Our next-door neighbor, Mister Cullison, eventually obtained permission to tear up the railroad tracks. He sawed the creosoted ties into small pieces. He had bushel baskets .We filled these with wood and sold them for 25 cents a basket or three baskets for 50 cents.

I suspect it's axiomatic that when you have a ghost, you must first have a dead person. At least that was how I felt when I was growing up and overheard the adults prattle on about 'crime'. These, it seemed, were mostly murders or accidental killings. I suspect that there is another truism at work here. People who have no work to keep them busy gossip a lot. One of the deaths they discussed happened to a relative of a relative. That was Merle Hankey. He was a brother of my Uncle, Dick Hankey. Dick had married my Mother's oldest sister, Mary. This murder evidently happened at a spot on West High Street which is the start of an alley running back of South Washington Street.

Merle Hankey had a fairly large family but, according to the adult gossip, it was rumored that Merle also had "outside' interests. He and another man got into a drunken brawl over a Lady who lived on West High Street. The other man hit Merle Hankey in the head with a brick and killed him.

Over time I came to know the remaining Hankeys. They, in fact, became my close friends. Mrs. Hankey, with the help of her young sons, kept the family together. Many of the boys served in World War II. After the war, they opened Hankey's Grocery at the corner of Washington and High Streets. This was just half a block from where Merle had been killed.

My Mother told me later that the man who killed Merle Hankey was caught and sent to jail. In jail he lost part of one foot in an accident. My Mother always shook her head as she explained. "I remember seeing him limping around the neighborhood after he got out. You could tell that part of his foot was gone." I'm not sure why, but that seemed to bother her more than Merle's death.

Also in our neighborhood lived a lady everybody called 'Aunt Bella'. Aunt Bella and her husband, Uncle Harv, had no children and were not related to us. But they were very generous people.. During the early days of World War II, they placed a huge church bench in front of their house. Every day, at noon, this bench was filled with men waiting to go inside to buy lunch for under a dollar. Aunt Bella home cooked a big meal, laid it all out on a table, and let the men take all they could eat. The men from the Panel and Furniture Factory would eat their lunch there. It wasn't exactly a legitimate restaurant but it served a good purpose. I suspect it also generated enough cash to furnish a good part of the family income.

I can still envision Uncle Harv. He was especially notable because he had lost a lot of fingers to the ripsaw he'd run in the Furniture Factory. Then, too, Uncle Harv always had a horse choking wad of tobacco in or around his mouth.

The scandal was about Aunt Bella's nephew who had been arrested for stealing 'a' chicken. He was sentenced to jail. Aunt Bella took in his wife and kids until he was released. Today, nobody would be sent to the jail for stealing 'a' chicken. I never found out but I suspected that he'd stolen 'a' chicken a time or two before. Perhaps the Judge who sentenced him was aware of this. Whatever the truth may be, Aunt Bella kept her nephew's family alive and well until her nephew was released.

Then, too, there was the shootout up at the AME Zion Church. This is a black church on the corner of Washington and Breckenridge Streets. A State cop was shot in the leg by another man. I don't know much about this incident other than that. But when I was growing up this story was a part of the verbal history of the Third Ward. There were lots of violent stories about life in the Third Ward. Most folks seemed to think this was because the Third Ward was the 'poor' ward and poor people resort more to direct action than to the law.

In one sense this was true. I knew a lot of 'poor' kids. I don't remember any of them coming from the First Ward; maybe a couple came from the Second Ward. The First Ward was Lincoln Avenue and Broadway. This is where the bankers, doctors, lawyers and the college professors lived. In other words, affluent white men lived in the First and Second Wards. But you should note that a lot of these relatively rich white men would visit the Cotton Club which was located in the Third Ward.

The Savoy Taproom was located on West High Street. It was a place where black men congregated to drink beer. There was never really any shortage of alcohol in Gettysburg. Despite prohibition, bootlegging had thrived, especially in the Third Ward. The Savoy Taproom also sponsored poker games. Along with the gambling, there were what we knew as 'high yellow ladies'. They entertained the visitors with a touch more than just song and dance

.

The Savoy Taproom was the locale for another Third Ward legend. One night, Mister Stanton, a black community leader, a veteran of World War I and a very successful businessman who owned his own house was shot to death during a poker game. The game had involved both black and white men. The man who shot Stanton was a white man from a prominent Gettysburg family. His brother was a well known local attorney. After the shooting, the killer left town, never to return by daylight. It's said he crept into town on occasion to visit with his family.

Mrs. Stanton was a friend of my Mother's. After the shooting, I remember going up to her house with my Mother and visiting the widow. Mrs. Stanton was left with two daughters she raised to be ladies. My Father claimed he knew the shooter. He told me he heard there had been a settlement designed to avoid prosecution. This apparently was a part of the cover-up which was much rumored in the Third Ward.

There is one more Third Ward story I heard from both my Father, and from the best man at my wedding. This concerned three men who apparently worked together as butchers. In those days in Gettysburg, animals were slaughtered in alleys behind the butcher shops. The entrails were placed in barrels, packed up and hauled off by a firm named 'Reese'. Reese was known as a 'bone and skin' company.

The three men were busy butchering a beef. A black man was aiding them. They send the black man out to buy a bottle of whiskey. He brought it back and the men took turns swigging down the liquor as they butchered the beef. There were no glasses. They just passed the bottle around. Whether he thought he was a part of the group or not, when it was passed to him, the black man took a swig directly from the bottle. The white man objected to this. There was an argument and the three white butchers killed the black man. The butchers then butchered the black man. They dismembered him and stuck the pieces in the rendering barrels. Mr. Reese took him away and treated the remains of his body like any other batch of entrails. The black man became part of the fertilizer spread over the Adams County farms.

The three white butchers eventually came to evil ends. The first committed suicide in the mid-thirties. Years later, the second ended up in the same alley behind the butcher shop with a rope around his neck. The third is rumored to have passed away in some equally violent, not described, manner.

In the Third Ward, most domestic disputes were never viewed as crimes. I don't remember anyone getting a divorce during the Depression. A divorce cost money. Money was scarce. There was no economic reason for most women to try and put a bite on her guy. He didn't have anything to give her. And vice versa. In those days if a man wanted to walk away from his wife and children, he just walked. They didn't even haul you in to court and make you pay for raising your kids. If you couldn't support them while you were married, how were you going to support them when you weren't? I've always figured that the primary reason for divorce in today's world, barring uncalled for cruelty or beatings, is to arrange the redistribution of assets.

What we heard in the Third Ward when I was growing up was "She's his housekeeper." There were a lot of women in the Third Ward who'd gone to housekeeping, and a lot of men who had housekeepers. As the gossip maintained, if the kids were grown and the ladies no longer cared that much for their legal mate, there was always a guy down the street who had a few more bucks. Under these circumstances no one even raised an eyebrow if the lady just walked out of the house and moved on down or up the street. So far as I know, no one was ever shot over such a situation.

Within the family, my paternal grandparents separated. My grandmother became a 'housekeeper' for a man down in New Oxford. There, evidently, was some acrimony between my grandparents over this, but I never witnessed it. Grandma said she had applied for the job because the man from New Oxford had put an ad in the paper. Whatever the arrangements actually were, in the family, we said Grandma had gone to 'housekeeping'.

When my grandfather was nearing death, my parents called grandmother who was still keeping house in New Oxford. She came in to Gettysburg to visit him. I was in the room when my grandfather died. This is an experience I've never forgotten. I was almost nine years old and my grandfather was the first person I'd ever watched die.

Granddad had a stroke several days before he passed on. I suspect they might have saved him today. He actually died at my Aunt's house at 44 South Street. My Aunt had taken him in because he'd fallen in the rooming house where he lived and nobody could afford to pay for a stay in the hospital.

My grandfather's name was Matthew Matthias Yingling. Everybody called him 'Mac'. That's the name on his tombstone: 'Mac Yingling'. When my grandmother walked into the room that fatal day, the first thing she said was, "Mac, let's have a cigarette together." My grandfather didn't smoke but grandma did. He roused enough to agree and they sat there smoking and made their peace. I figured this was like Indians smoking a peace pipe. There was not a lot of puffing, just a lot of silence and a bit of ceremony. Even at my tender age, I understood this to be proper between them.

The two of them had not spoken in at least four years. My Dad had always avoided taking sides. He loved both his parents. Both were always welcome at our house. If my grandmother was there and

Grandpa showed up, he'd keep right on going out the backdoor. Granddad was almost totally blind when he died. I still have his white cane.

The had been in their fifties when he first accused her of cheating and they separated. Like my Dad, I loved both of them. Grandmother would give you anything she had to give and my grandfather was just plain wonderful to be around. Their children were out of the house so what was anyone to blame them for.

When she moved out, granddad transferred their house over to my Father. Eventually, the house was sold and the proceeds were split equally between them. It probably wasn't much, only a couple of hundred for each.

I was happy they'd made peace with each other before he died. I don't remember that grandmother even came to his funeral. But that was not a problem for the family. The two of them had made peace with each other before he died. That was the important memory for all of us to hold on to.

In retrospect, the truth is that the late Thirties were an unsettled time for many people. Today, we refer to a lot of familial unease as 'the midlife crisis'. Today, mostly it's men who go flaky in their 40's. Back then, I think more women jumped ship. Even today, I've heard women refer to the situation as 'getting liberated'. During the early Forties this urge for liberation was called 'the itch'. During World War II many husbands went off to war and many women scratched that itch. What those of us sequestered in the Third Ward believed was a local phenomenon turned out to be a national sickness.

As I mentioned previously, the big family event for me was my getting to name my newly born twin brother and sister. Picking 'Mark Joseph' from the New Testament was an easy choice for an Altar Boy. 'Ave' came from my admiration of a family member named Miss Ave Maria Rosensteel.

A FEW THOUGHTS ABOUT WORLD WAR II

The CCC had taught me a lot about national organizations, as had the PWA and later, its successor, the WPA. But along with these jobs oriented groups, I was also very much aware of the military. There were federally funded and sponsored military organizations like the Civilian Military Training Corps (CMTC). Initially, a lot of these were located on college campuses. Later, they were mostly replaced by direct military groups such as the Air Cadets. This made an early appearance on the Gettysburg College Campus. When I was delivering papers, I used to pass right through their area.

Joining the military before the war actually broke out was almost always a matter of needing three square meals a day. Even though the money wasn't much, a recruit still had a place to sleep, food to eat, and good new clothes.

As kids, we used to play army. You have to understand that we kids never fought the Japanese, or the Germans, or any other government we'd ever heard of. We didn't even re-fight the Civil War. We didn't play Yankees fighting Johnny Reb, even though the history of that conflict was all about us. We just picked two sides and called ourselves armies. Lots of times we turned branches into guns and did a whole lot of make believe shooting. I guess that all turned real for us when our first family member was called up in the early draft. That was Luther Grimes, one of my Mother's younger brothers.

Luther was drafted early in 1941 on his 21st birthday. He was in so early that he saw service in both North Africa and Europe. He went all through the war and didn't get discharged until 1946. He never came home to find out his wife had been entertaining the home troops. When he finally did, he divorced her, re-upped for the army and ultimately remarried. I was enchanted by Luther's tales of his service. "I was attached to Patton's tank corp. I drove a supply truck. We got strafed by the Germans. One time a truck was blown up right in front of me. The blast disintegrated everybody on board. There was blood and guts everywhere. It was all over everything. . Everybody just disintegrated." I was fascinated by the idea that people could get disintegrated that way.

I remember Pearl Harbor Day, December 7, 1941. We had driven up to Carlisle to visit Grandpa and Grandma Grimes at their farm. They were my Mother's parents. It was family custom for us to spend a day with them every month or six weeks. We started back late afternoon and didn't stop until we crossed the railroad tracks which passed over Carlisle Road. Dad was getting low on gas at that point so he stopped at the first gas station he saw after the tracks. Dad wanted a dollar's worth of gas. At that time a dollar bought at least three and maybe four gallons.

"Did you folks hear about those stinking Japs attacking Pearl Harbor?" The gas station attendant was all riled up. I didn't exactly understand the full significance of the question but Dad responded quietly.

"Well, I guess Mister Roosevelt got his wish. I guess that bombing means we're gonna get into the war in Europe now." I remember that my Father seemed both excited and quietly perturbed at the same time. He definitely did not look too happy at the news.

My Father was dead right even though I had trouble figuring out what an attack by the Japanese on Hawaii had to do with us fight in Europe. I was only eleven and not a candidate to go into the military. But, as it turned out, I did know a whole bunch of people who were candidates and did go. News items about warriors like Colin Kelly excited me, and everybody I knew.

As the war years ground on, four men I knew personally went off to war and got themselves killed. They all lived within a block of our house on Washington Street. The first one I learned of was Mister Smith. He lived catercornered across the street, maybe three or four houses up. He was 20 years old and a staff sergeant when he was killed in Europe. I had talked with him one time when he was home on leave. I was just a kid and he didn't need to spend time with me, but he did. He even patted me on the head when he was called back into the house.

Morris Small lived just five doors down from us. He was the oldest of 12 children and now there are only 2 still living. Chet, the youngest son, still runs The Horse Soldier, a shop in Gettysburg. Morris was the oldest child but was not drafted until they were getting ready for the push in Europe and D-Day. Then, they apparently needed more troops. I figure Morris got caught in what was almost the last full scale draft. Morris was 35 when he was finally drafted. That scared me a bit. My Dad was only 42. He had had to register for the draft despite his age and having 3 children. With Morris having to go I feared my Father might be called next. But that never happened.

As it turned out, every one of the Small boys served in World War II except Chet. Like me, Chet was too young. At one time the Smalls had five sons in service: Morris, Barney, Bill, Tub and Phillip. Morris was married to a good looking woman named Martha but they didn't have children. Morris was killed in Europe. Martha died soon after. My Mother told me it was of a broken heart.

After the Smalls moved off the block, the Barr family moved in. Their son had been a gunner and was shot down in combat. It turned out that the son's wife and twin girls were living with the Barr family. Paul Barr, who also went to the Parochial School, was my age. He told me the twin girls had been born on the day their father was shot down. Their Mother was a very attractive lady, so I wasn't surprised to hear later that she'd remarried and moved to Delaware.

The Dorsey family were black. They lived right around the corner from us. Their son, Duke, was one hell of a high school athlete. We heard that he'd been killed on a mine tender during the height of the war.

There were other men from Gettysburg killed or wounded during World War II, but I'm not aware that any other single block was so heavily impacted. Conversely, so far as I recall, my own family suffered no catastrophic losses.

I've been surprised to find that many of my friends are not aware of the role kids played in World War II. A lot of them were too young to even be working at the time, and many others were in the armed forces and unaware of what was happening at home.

For my part, I collected a number of earned medals. For example, since I was a carrier for the Gettysburg Times, I participated in the program whereby the carriers sold war savings stamps and bonds. I had 165 customers and earned a dollar seventy-five cents a week. I banked every cent of that except for perhaps a quarter.

I always knocked on my customer's doors and asked, "How about buying some war stamps today?" I was seldom refused. For this effort I received medals. I also received the Eisenhower Medal for selling War Bonds. Would you believe I still have all those medals.

I also collected scrap newspapers and sold these at Morris Gitling's junkyard. This money also went directly into the bank. Beyond the newspaper business, I also picked cherries, peaches and apples in county orchards where the usual laborers were off to war. I received a special commendation from the Department of Agriculture for that contribution to the war effort. In a sense my contribution to the war effort was small potatoes, but I was just eleven when the conflict started and still under 16 when it ended. In that sense, I suspect I did what I could to help out. As we all realize now, World War II was perhaps the defining moment of many of our lives.

If my kids ever think to ask me what I did during World War II, I don't mind telling them that I sold war stamps and bonds, that I picked cherries, peaches and apples, and that I rounded up scrap to sell to Morris Gittling's junkyard.

GETTYSBURG COLLEGE

In the fall of 1949, when I entered Gettysburg College, I was eighteen years old and no idea of what communism was really all about. Joe McCarthy's complaints about the State Department being riddled with communists rolled off me like water off a duck. When Truman ordered the Atomic Energy Commission to develop a hydrogen bomb I understood nothing of the implications.

Thanks again to my Mother, I entered Gettysburg College as a full fledged Sophomore. I lived at home that year and didn't work fulltime. Even now, it seems like a dream. I was able to meet a lot of people and make a lot of friends. I became active in the ATO fraternity and participated fully in the social and community program of the college. I did work during that sophomore year but it was on the weekends and not as wearing as later jobs would prove to be.

On weekends I washed dishes at the Gettysburg Hotel and served as an usher and ticket-taker at the local theater. A fellow classmate was the manager of the Strand Theater. This was Dean Stultz. Dean had been ahead of me in High School, but he knew I was also local.

During my junior and senior years it was back to the grind. I carried between 15 and 18 hours per semester. I once again needed money, so I held down a full time job at the Rubber Heel Factory. I worked the night shift, 11 at night till 7 in the morning. I averaged four hours sleep per week day. That wiped out any chance of participating in extra curricular activities at the College.

In truth, there was another reason I took the job at the Rubber Heel. I didn't just need money for College. I needed it to support my marriage. In 1951 when I was twenty, I went home one afternoon and told my Dad that Genny Koontz and I were going to get married.

My Father never questioned my decision. After going steady for two years, we had become engaged the previous Christmas so he'd had some warning.

"Jakey, make me one promise. Promise me you'll finish college."

"I will." I said, knowing full well that was a promise I'd never dare break. I worked, and Genny also continued to work at the phone company.

At that time, the strongest academic departments at Gettysburg College were history and chemistry. Doctor Fortenbaugh was Head of the History Department and my advisor. He was the professor who had the strongest influence on me at Gettysburg. I was a history major but had to take multiple education courses to get my teaching permit. I regret to say that Education seemed to be the weakest department on campus. I felt no need to pay tuition to learn how to operate a film or slide projector. Indeed, some of the Education courses were an outright waste of time, money and energy. I hope they've strengthened their course since then.

Doctor Glatfelter was new at Gettysburg when I arrived. Eventually, he became head of the History Department. My first course with him was Political Science. Doctor Glatfelter is now head of the Adams County Historical Society. On a visit to the Society in 1999, I asked him why he didn't give me an 'A' in his class.

"I always made an 'A' on your tests. I wrote good papers and I listened to every word of your lectures.:

"Mister Yingling!" He replied in that well known gravely voice. "Count your blessings. It's impossible to give an 'A' to a student who sits in the back row and sleeps through most of the class. Besides, you snored right out loud. That was downright disruptive." I didn't remind him that he'd known right up front that I worked all night every night making rubber heels.

In this context, it is ironic that, prior to the meeting with Doctor Glatfelter at the Adams County Historical Society, I had completed my term of office as President of the Carroll County Historical Society in Westminster, Maryland. Election to that office had come about because of many years of support to the organization, my legislative activities and, I suspect, because of one speech I delivered in 1970 which received good press coverage.

This speech concerned Abraham Lincoln and was given on the occasion of Lincoln's birthday. On at least one occasion, a similar speech was redelivered by Joe Getty, another member of the Maryland legislature and also a member of the historical society. Then, my speech was researched and became a feature article in the Carroll County Times. The latter was prepared by Jay Graybeal, current Director of the Historical Society.

A. Jake and Genny married on April 5, 1951.
B. Rosie Koontz, Genny's Mom.

A. Matthew 'Mack' Yingling and Lillie Mae Weikert.
B. Jake, Dad, Mom, and Ave on Ave's Wedding day.

**Genny's Mom holding Genny sitting beside her Sisters
Anna Belle, Romaine, and Loretta.**

GENNY SPEAKS OUT

I was born one month and three days before Jake. That was on August 27, 1930. He was born in Aspers, PA and I was born in Knoxlyn, another small community just outside Gettysburg. Had you asked me at age ten if I'd end up marrying a boy from Gettysburg, a college boy no less, I'd have just laughed at what I would have seen as a preposterous thought. My early world encompassed the farm, the church and the family.

At that time, we lived on what you might call a 'hardscrabble farm'. My mother and father moved there in 1929. I was one of eleven children. My favorite sister was Laureen. She was ten years older than me and may have been the one who first started calling me 'Snooky'. 'Snooky' became my family name.

Before moving to the farm, my family had lived on Steinwehr Avenue in Gettysburg. That was where I believe some of my older sisters were born. Some of them were old enough to have been my mother. Others may have been born in a weathered clapboard house out on Taneytown Road.. Many years later, when I first applied for a passport, I discovered that I didn't even have a registered birth certificate. In those days, farm births tended to be less noted events than those accomplished in the hospital.

Life on the farm was difficult. We had no running water, nor any electricity. My mother scrubbed clothes on a rubber washing pad and hung them out to dry. The white things were mostly first boiled in big black kettles. Beyond laundry, my mother was kept busy canning, cleaning and caring for the kids. She helped tend the garden for good measure.

My father always juggled several jobs. At one time or another he worked in a brickyard out on York Road. I am aware that he helped build the Pennsylvania monument in the Military Cemetery. Later, he held several jobs as a furnace stoker ('fireman' as they called it then) and as a night watchman. He also worked at the Rubber Heel with two sons and one son-in-law. Jake even worked there at a much later date.

From one point of view, 'Food', the farm was an ideal place to be during the Depression. The family had very little cash and nothing fancy in the way of furniture or clothes, but we never went hungry. We had two cows and raised hogs. We butchered and dressed our own hogs. We canned all the fruit and vegetables that came to hand. Mom milked cows and made her own butter. Every weekend she baked eight to nine pies. We had no car but my Aunts and Uncles all came to Daddy's place every Sunday. That was after church.

One hard and fast rule was that we must go to Church and Sunday School every Sunday. While living on the farm, we attended the Church of the Brethren at Lower Marsh Creek. Most of the attendees were must like my parents. They were God-fearing, land loving conservative leaning farm folk.

We lived on the farm at Knoxlyn until I was in the middle of the sixth grade. At that time the family, five girls and Mom and Dad, moved into a house at 118 Carlisle Street. This was right across the street from what is now Monahan's Mortuary. At that time it was Bender's Funeral Home.

Since I wanted to finish the sixth grade in the one room school I attended, I stayed with my sister Hilda until I finished up. In truth, I was a bit afraid that I would be too far behind the city crowd, having always attended the same one room school. Hazel Carson taught all subjects in all eight grades. But I was wrong to worry. Miss Hazel had done her job well, very well as it turned out.

I signed into the seventh grade at the Lincoln School in Gettysburg, a public school. I attended Lincoln until I enrolled at Gettysburg High where my world immediately broadened. I was invited to sing in the choir at the Reform Church. Eventually I joined the Reform Church, but I also often went to St. James Lutheran with my mother. During this time, things picked up a bit for Dad and he bought a house on Middle Street. I can still remember how proud he was of that house. I think its ownership represented more of an achievement to him then I really understood at the time. Unfortunately, my Dad died when I was almost fifteen.

My father was sixty-five when he suffered a massive stroke. Seven days later he passed away. My only consolation is that while my father death came after a hard, hard life, he died a much loved man. Eleven children, one lifelong wife and many, many friends will testify to that.

As for me, I had a ball in High School. I played on the basketball and volleyball squads and began to get a feel for the huge world which I'd barely encountered as a kid growing up on an isolated farm. Indirectly, it was my playing high school sports which led me to Jake. But our contacts were casual at first and each of us was dating someone else when we met. It was only on the senior trip to Washington that I got to know him as a person. Later, my mother became very fond of Jake. That helped, especially since I was aware that my mother had run off a couple of my sister's dates that she hadn't cared for.

My first real job was with Glenn L. Brame, the Cadillac Dealer. After graduating from high school, I was fortunate to procure a job at the United Telephone Company. Sister Laureen had told me she'd pay my way through nursing school, but at age seventeen and right out of school, I was suddenly making a surprising amount of money and working at a job I loved. I just couldn't abandon that. It was manual ringing and all that repetitive talking, but, basically, being an operator was a very good job with nice people in a pleasant surrounding.

Gradually, Jake and I became closer. We were married on April 5, 1951 at the Rectory of St. Francis Xavier Church. The only proviso I can recall anybody making came from Jake's father. "Jakey, you must finish college." We, certainly, both agreed with that.

At the time of our wedding, we were both about twenty and a half and neither of us had much money. I went back to work at the phone company while Jake stayed on at Gettysburg College until he graduated.

I continued to work at the phone company up until two weeks before our oldest boy, Stephen Jacob, was born. Unlike me, Stevie had the full attention of a hospital staff and an attending physician, Doctor D. C. Stoner. It was a blessing that we were living with Jake's parents at this time and his mother could help with Stevie.

Indeed, Emma stayed with Stevie between my shifts even though I slipped home to feed him whenever I could. Emma's cooperation enabled me to return to work about two weeks later and to save the money which ultimately bought us our first furniture at Raymond's Home Furnishings. At that time we lived at 338 S. Washington Street.

Later, we moved into a house on Baltimore Street. I remember Jake's fraternity brothers coming down to see Stevie while we were still at Washington Street. Jake was the only married member of his fraternity and his brothers were impressed with Stevie. That was my strongest memory of Washington Street. What I remember most about Baltimore Street is that Jake bought a little red wagon in which he used to ride Stevie up and down the hill.

I continued to work until we moved to Westminster. There, I did not hold a full time job but I did teach at the YMCA sponsored Chipmunk program at the Methodist Church. Unfortunately, the YMCA Supervisor from Baltimore insisted that we three teachers all had to take training in Early Childhood Education. We quit at the end of the program instead, and I settled in to become a stay at home Mom. In 1959 we had a second son, Randall Matthew. He was born on July 7th.

The eight year difference in age made a difference in the sports scene in Westminster. Stevie was just four when we moved to Westminster and the little leagues, which became important a part of their lives, were just forming. When Randy came along they had achieved a comparatively sophisticated level and the coaching was much stronger. Both boys also joined cub scouts but they preferred little league baseball. They each lettered in High School Lacrosse and Football. At one point, Steve even coached Randy in lacrosse. When I look back at how Jake had originally wanted to coach football and teach, Steve's doing this seemed like the belated realization of a dream.

Randy was less picky about food than Steve, but he did develop an aversion to eggs when he was involved in a grade school research project. After finding out where peeps came from, he'd been totally turned off. For his part, Steve wanted nothing to do with meat loaf or vegetable soup. On the other hand, Steve loved potato salad.

At this time we were living in a home we'd built on Washington Road. That house cost us $12,000. Later on, in 1959, we moved to William Avenue where Randy grew up. In 1974 we made the move to our current home on Kalten Road.

Steve was offered a scholarship from the University of Virginia but turned that down to go to Gettysburg College. Partly, this was influenced by Jake's former coach, Mister Shoemaker, or 'Shoey', as Jake always called him. Randy later had a scholarship offer for Lacrosse at Ohio State which he also turned down also in favor of Gettysburg.

During the boy's growing up years, we made a lot of automobile trips to places like Erie and Niagara Falls. Jake took each boy on one air trip. Steve accompanied him to Charleston, West Virginia where Jake was speaking at a conference. Randy went on a trip to San Antonio, Texas where Jake was working with the San Antonio Police Department. A Lieutenant from the Police Department took both of them over the border into Mexico. Jake had been asked to try and get some Mexican gold pesos. That trip turned into a real fiasco.

When they all went into the bank, dressed in suits as they were, they were mistaken for robbers who had held up the bank two weeks before. Recently hired armed guards leveled their guns and threatened to shoot them. It took quite a while for the Lieutenant to extradite them from the clutches of the Mexican lawmen.

Steve and Randy both grew up under strict family rules. One of these said that they had to be physically in the house by eleven. Jake was a strict disciplinarian when it came to this. He even went out looking for Steve one night when he was late. Their reactions to us as parents were always different. Steve mostly internalized things and it wasn't always easy to know what he was thinking. Randy was always right out in broad daylight. He couldn't hold a secret if revealing it would kill him. I think that continues right up until today. Steve is still reserved while Randy is much more outgoing.. This all part of their personalities and my comment is not critical. It is just a part of understanding the boys.

Both of our boys were baptized Catholic. Steve was baptized in Gettysburg at St. Francis Xavier while Randy was baptized in Westminster at St. John's. I had converted to Catholicism in 1959. Steve married into a family which is half-Catholic and half-Protestant.

Randy is more Lutheran. Jake and I eventually left St. John's and became members of the Lutheran church we attend today.

Randy was the first to marry. He and Marianne Miller of Cherry Hill, N.J. were married on January 23, 1982, the stormiest day anyone could have selected for a formal event. They have two children: a son, Tyler Barrett, born on July 1, 1985, and a daughter, Randall Morgan, born on September 23, 1988.

Steve met his wife, Cindy Eni of Medford Lakes, N. J. at Randy and Marianne's wedding. Cindy had been a roommate's of Marianne's at Gettysburg. A year and a half later, Steve and Cindy were married on June 23, 1984. Steve and Cindy have three sons: Christopher Stephen, born January 8, 1987; Timothy Andrew, born January 29, 1991; and Gregory Scott, born January 25, 1993.

PART FOUR:
STARTING A CAREER
A DOG HELPED ME WIN
ACQUIN FEENEY
RANDOM HOUSE NEGOTIATION
MY SECOND RUN FOR OFFICE
THE LEGISLATURE GRINDS ON
WESTINGHOUSE LEARNING

Randy and Marianne on their Wedding day.

Emma, Cindi, and Steve on Steve and Cindi's Wedding day.

The Grandchildren: from the top: Timmy, Chris, Greg, Tyler, and Randall.

STARTING A CAREER

As Charles Dickens would have it, when I graduated from College it was the best of times and the worst of times to be tossed out into the cold cruel world. I graduated from Gettysburg College in 1952. The previous year I had been slightly shocked when McArthur was relieved of the Far East Command after the North Korean forces broke through at the 38th Parallel. In truth, Eisenhower had been my long time hero, but I admired McArthur's arrogant posture and stage presence. It was interesting to me that following this, Eisenhower was elected to the Presidency.

Like most of my friends I moved out into the world without the succor of a family business to run to. Additionally, I had a wife and a child to support. Therefore, I was forced to utilize a skill I had worked with long and hard for many years. I turned to selling.

There had been no time to hesitate. As a married man, I felt I needed to support my wife and young son better than I had been able to while a college student. The job I took sent me out to sell insurance for a fraternal organization. The customers were almost like my newspaper people. They were members of the fraternal organization and easily identifiable. I had learned early on to always ask for the order so I did well. That first year out of college I managed to save $1,700.

On the other hand, there were two problems with that insurance job. First of all, the constant travel prevented me from establishing roots and having sufficient time at home with my family. Secondly, I had trained to be a teacher. I liked the idea of teaching. Also, I had been sure I'd have no trouble getting a job teaching. That desire to teach was a kind of nagging, annoying ideal.

At the end of my first year selling, I applied for a teaching job only to find there were no openings in the Gettysburg area. Rather than go back on the road, I took a job at Shepherd Diesel which was located in Hanover, PA. This is a town just east of Gettysburg. At the Diesel works, I learned to operate a boring mill. My job was to take iron castings and grind out the fuel pump, the main bearing, and the camshaft. These became motor parts for diesel powered tractors. I learned quickly and soon became able to set up jobs on my own.

In August of 1954, now two years out of Gettysburg College, I told my boss at the diesel works that I was going to leave. I said that I had been offered a job teaching school.

"How in hell can you do that?" he asked, completely baffled. "You have to have a college degree to teach school."

"I'm sorry." I replied with considerable embarrassment. I had never owned up to having a college degree because I had been warned that they might not hire me. "I hope you'll forgive me for not filling out the form completely."

"Nah! That's OK. Now I understand why you were able to read prints and set up your own jobs with so little work background."

I was slightly frustrated that the teaching job I'd obtained was not in Pennsylvania. However, it was next door in the town of Manchester Maryland. Manchester is just over the Mason Dixon Line. I became a core teacher at Manchester Elementary and Middle School. This means I taught everything but math and science.

I commuted from Gettysburg and, at the start, had no intention of moving to Maryland. That change came later when I switched from teaching to work in the textbook publishing industry. Then, the job required me to move inside my territory.

Starting off commuting as I did turned out to be a very happy circumstance. I met Mister Charles Briton. He, also, was commuting from Gettysburg to teach Manchester. We shared rides and swapped tales ad infinitum. My only problem was that despite his request that I call him 'Charlie', I had trouble addressing him as anything other than 'Mister Briton'. That was the inbred courtesy I'd learned at my Mother's knee and sitting on the courthouse wall with my Father.

Mister Briton had retired in Pennsylvania as a School Superintendent but still wanted to teach. He'd found work teaching math at Manchester High School while I'd landed at the Junior High School.

Sometimes you meet people who, for no real reason, like you and enable changes which affect the direction of your entire life. They contribute to your ultimate success with good counsel and a few introductions. Mister Briton, for me, was one of those people. I owe him lot. He was directly responsible for the move which really launched my career.

Every fall the Maryland Teacher's Association held a large meeting and textbook exhibit in Baltimore. Mister Briton and I attended the exhibit together. In the exhibit hall, Mister Briton ran into an old friend, Norm Seiple. Norm Seiple was a bookman (textbook salesman) who used to call on Mister Briton when he was a School Administrator.

"I'm moving on, Charlie." announced Norm Seiple. "I've been promoted to Regional Manager. Hey, I have a thought. You know a lot of teachers in both Pennsylvania and Maryland. Do you know anyone with both sales and teaching experience? Is there anyone you'd recommend as a textbook salesman for our Maryland/DC territory?"

Mister Briton didn't even hesitate. "Norm," he said. "I have the perfect candidate for you."

After hearing what Mister Briton had to say about me as a person and about my sales background, Norm Seiple interviewed me exhaustively. Then, he made an offer I just couldn't refuse.

"You'll get an expense account and a company car. We'll start you right now at more money than you'll ever make teaching."

"Look, Mister Seiple." I replied. "I want the job, but I'm in my first year of teaching. I'm under contract."

"Leave that to me, Jake. I know exactly how to handle the situation." And he did.

Norm Seiple went to see Sam Jenness who, at that time, was Superintendent of Carroll County Schools. Sam recognized what an opportunity this was for me. He told Norm he felt sure he could fill the vacancy. I was permitted to resign at midyear. In those days, most schoolbook salesmen were ex-principals or school administrators. At that time, textbook selling was a comparatively lucrative job. Many salesmen were making more money than the Superintendents of the Districts in their territory. I know I was only given consideration because of the strength of Mister Briton's recommendation.

Mister Briton later died of cancer. He was loved and missed by everyone who knew him. His recommendation changed the direction of my life and decreed my fortuitous move to Maryland.

I say 'fortuitous' because the move gave me an opportunity to begin anew in a way that would have been exceedingly difficult in Gettysburg. Once I had left that environment, I understood why I had so much trouble getting a teaching job there. For one thing, my family had no connections with the real decision makers, the ones who thought of themselves as 'movers and shakers'. Whether I liked it or not, I had been labeled 'Third Ward'.

I also say 'fortuitous' because a textbook salesman sees every part of his territory in an objective manner. Sooner or later he meets everyone who is anyone in Education. More than that, he is exposed in a non-confrontational way to how people think and feel about issues, not just educational issues, but every issue which impacts their lives.

What is even more fortuitous about the situation is that a textbook salesman has time on his side. He can work way on beyond the normal closing of the day, or he can leave early – just so long as he is producing. This provides the one thing most 'employees' don't have built into their jobs – time to think and study what is going on about them.

I've always been an avid newspaper reader so I started almost at once to read local papers comprehensively in order to build a political sense about my new Town, County and State. Gettysburg, while no further from Harrisburg, the state capital, than Westminster was from Annapolis, had seemed inclined to focus more heavily on local issues. To the people I contacted in Maryland, the Baltimore Sun and the Washington Post seemed more important sources. In Gettysburg I had almost never read the Pittsburgh, Harrisburg or Philadelphia papers.

Regionally reported items which I encountered included the fact that the Chesapeake Bridge had opened in 1952. Historic Annapolis, Inc. had been founded that same year. This tweaked my historic bent. Johns Hopkins Hospital had opened the nations first intensive care facility. In 1953, the local papers focused their attention on Brown vs. The Board of Education case as it was led by a combination of Thurgood Marshall and the NAACP. Everyone in the education field watched with interest as they won the decision in the following year. Also, in 1954, Baltimore schools desegregated and University of Maryland integrated. This was the first state university south of the Mason Dixon line to do so.

Two other events which occurred in this same time span were to have great significance to me. The first black was elected to the Maryland House of Delegates and the Baltimore Washington Expressway opened. The first was important because it told me that attitudes in Maryland were indeed more liberal than those I'd grown up with. And with a sales territory which included the District of Columbia, I truly needed a faster route between Baltimore and Washington.

As is true of any salesman, I spent a lot of time waiting for other people to see me. I didn't waste that time. When I didn't have reports to prepare and file, I read! I put myself through a Graduate Level Course which some of my friends have called 'Newspaper Immersion 101'.

Prior to my own first run for office I caught up with Maryland's daily life and with its history. In 1955, I read all about the crisis in Montgomery, Alabama as Rosa Parks inadvertently became a leader of the bus boycott. At the same time, a friend of mine from another textbook company was sent to Alabama by the American Textbook Institute to gather information about a proposed law that would have outlawed any textbook mention of Civil Rights and everything which surrounded the idea. He was not welcomed with open arms. [But he did find a few friendly legislators and the bill failed on the first reading.]

Along with the accidental research into what would become sustenance for my later work in the Legislature I became very active in a number of civic and church organizations. Then I made a fateful decision. I decided to run for a seat in the Maryland Legislature.

At that moment I was still not sure I had all the ingredients needed for making the run, but I had invested eight years in service to my community. My only brochure was a one page flyer. This listed my reasons for running as well as a list of my accomplishments. Included were: my education and my family and an indication of how active I had been in both Church and Civic Affairs.

I was President of the Westminster Babe Ruth League for three years. I was President of the Kiwanis Club. I had taught school in Manchester. I was Past Secretary and Treasurer of the Maryland, Delaware and District of Columbia Educational Salesman's Assoc, and was presently associated with the L. W. Singer Company, the textbook division of Random House. I had been the 1962 Chairman of the Carroll County Cancer Drive and currently was Treasurer of the Westminster Interdenominational Group.

Most importantly of all, I felt I had an honest message for the voters, one which justified my running for the House of Delegates. I quote from that first flyer.

Sooner than most people realize, you will be faced with the responsibility of selecting the people who will represent you in the House of Delegates in Annapolis. In order to fulfill this obligation, I realize it is necessary to know all you can about the candidates so you can select the ones who will best serve the interests of our county and state.

I would like to say that public service is my chief concern. I will not be indifferent to the public needs of my community, county and state. I, also, realize integrity, character and principle are the price that freedom exacts. I will not compromise with what I know to be wrong. My aim is to provide as well as to follow sound leadership. Education and instruction provide better understanding. I feel it is my duty as a citizen to do all I can to promote better understanding through education and instruction. I feel that faith in my fellow man, the courage of my convictions, common sense and trust in God are the necessary tools by which I can best serve you and our country. If elected to the House of Delegates I will never forget the trust that has been bestowed on me. I will be of service to all the people and to all areas of Carroll County.

My work schedule, which basically paralleled the school year, enabled me to run for the Legislature. I had the time to run and to serve if elected. Beyond this, in those days, the Legislature did not pay much money so the competition to serve was less.

A DOG HELPED ME WIN

One of those friends mentioned above lived in Union Bridge, Maryland. This was Harvey White. I had met Harvey and his sister at Gettysburg College. Harvey was four years older than me, but was at the college at the same time after serving in World War II. We were both members of the ATO fraternity. During my first campaign, which occurred in 1962, Harvey was employed at the Lehigh Cement Plant in Union Bridge. Because of our old school ties, he decided to help with my election effort.

Unlike the majority of Carroll County Towns, Union Bridge was a Democratic area. A member of the Democratic State Central Committee lived in the area and was one of the principals in the Democratic Advocate newspaper. I was running as a Republican.

After the election, I reviewed the returns and was slightly surprised to find that, against all odds, in Union Bridge I'd pulled the highest vote of any of the eight candidates for the Legislature. I remained surprised until I later received an explanatory call from Harvey.

"Hey, Jake." he said with a smile showing in his voice. "We did alright in Union Bridge."

"How did it happen?"

"Jake," he laughed. "It's a long story about a short haired dog." I waited while he teased me by not immediately continuing. Finally, I demanded the story.

"Wail, hail." He said. "It's like this. We have a black gentleman lives here, name of Robert Jones. His wife occasionally does work for us. When Mister Jones came to pick her up, he spotted our short hair German pointer. He just plain fell in love with that dog. He said to me, "Mr. White, I'd just love to have a dog like that.""

I had no idea where Harvey was going with this story, but I urged him to continue.

"I told Mister Jones that if he'd tell all his friends to vote for Jake Yingling, and he led the ticket, I'd give him the dog." When we both stopped laughing, Harvey finished his story.

"Well, Jake, you won the election and I don't have a short haired German pointer dog anymore, but Mister Jones is absolutely impressed with his own power to elect an official member of the legislature."

It should be noted that the Jones political tradition continues. Mister Jones' nephew became the mayor of Union Bridge, presumably with his uncle's help

Winning that election opened a whole new world to me and gave me a chance to see how a state government really works. That was an experience I wouldn't have missed for the world.

A. Senator Glenn Beale Sr. holding Randy.
B. Jake at his desk in Annapolis.

Randy on Jake's lap during a legislative session.
Jake with Brooks at Kiwanis Club.
Jake with friends.

The proud Grandparents.

Board of Directors of Westminster Trust, 1966
Front: Kale Mathias, Walter Warehime, Jim Schilling,
        Alvie Sprinkle, and Paul Kuhns
Back: Jake   Yingling,   Randall   Sporline,   John
       Schaeffer, Bob Jones, and Marlin Rittace

ACQUIN FEENEY

My election to the legislature expanded my horizons greatly, but so did the advice and aid I received from **ACQUIN FEENEY,** a seemingly unpretentious, but brilliant man with strong political and financial connections.

I met Ac Feeney in 1963. This was the same year John Kennedy was assassinated by Lee Harvey Oswald and replaced in the Presidency by Lyndon Johnson.

(Once again, a curious reader might care to play the infamous 'What if?' game. What if JFK had not been killed and Johnson never acceded to the Presidency. Then consider this. The assassination took place in Texas. Wouldn't it be logical for Lyndon Johnson to have been in the same limousine? What if he too had been killed? Who, then, would have become President? Personally, I think the cracks in Kennedy's armor were beginning to show and he was becoming vulnerable to same type of assaults recently leveled at Bill Clinton. On the other hand, even as a long time Republican, I believe Johnson's presidency worked to the ultimate good of the people. On the other hand, would another president have handled Vietnam better?)

I can set all speculation aside as to what have occurred had I not met Ac Feeney. My life would have been considerably poorer for his absence. Ac took an immediate interest in me and I was able to reciprocate by presenting some business situations I felt he might wish to explore.

He suggested in return that I get real estate and security licenses. These, he pointed out, would permit me to participate in opportunities which otherwise would be closed to me. As we talked, I learned that Ac Feeney had real estate businesses in both Baltimore and Carroll Counties.

As a young man growing up during the Depression, even with a law degree, Ac Feeney had had trouble finding a job. He took an interim job teaching at McDonogh, a private school just outside Baltimore. One of his students was Ben Raskob whose father was John Jacob Raskob.

Mister Raskob was in league with the top business and financial leaders of the Twenties. He was VP and Chairman of the finance committee or General Motors. John Jacob Raskob was also a member of the board and on the finance committee of Dupont. He was also a director of several New York banks.

In 1928, Al Smith ran for the presidency against Herbert Hoover. He selected John Jacob Raskob as chairman of the Democratic Party. In other words, Ben Raskob's father was a big time mover and shaker. He was also astute about money and had survived the Stock Market

Crash of 1929 unharmed. Best of all, John Jacob Raskob had been impressed with Ac Feeney and had hired him.

During the 1930's, Ac was Raskob's representative in Nevada where General Motors and Raskob both had large land and mining interests. Later, I met the son, Ben Raskob at his corporate headquarters in Albuquerque, New Mexico.

Ac Feeney died in 1980. Prior to that, he had introduced me to the principals of Equitable Bank and recommended that I serve on their advisory board. He did the same thing with St. Joseph's Hospital. On his recommendation, I was given a chance to serve on the hospital board with some of the top political and financial leaders in Maryland.

AC was involved in many other business activities. From time to time, he invited me to participate in these. People often ask me how I was able to work for a publisher, be a member of the legislature, and still participate in all these external activities. The answer is simple. As a textbook salesman, I had my summers free, plus long vacations at Christmas and other times when the schools were closed.

The other answer is that Ac Feeney took care to guide my activities. He saw that I was well briefed on the role I was to play in business negotiations. Ac Feeney played a tremendous role in my life. He exposed me to people I otherwise never would have met. He gave me opportunities that logically never would have existed had he not created them. Ac was a humble man with formidable contacts. He used these, not just to advocate his own goals, but also to help other people.

In many ways, my work with Ac Feeney exposed me to organizations as a topnotch consultant might see them. A close friend of mine who has functioned often in that capacity avers that: "All organizations are evil. And the older the organization, the more evil the organization inevitably will become."

My friend maintains that this theory pertains to all organizations: churches, political parties, governments and businesses of all kinds. I don't necessarily agree completely with this, but I can't really fight his contention that undue rigidity, lack of humanity, and the ability of individuals to commit crimes under the guise of achieving their organizational goals do exist. I certainly have personally observed much of this in banks, corporations and governments. I have functioned at relatively high and relatively low levels within each.

:'Morality', as most people understand the word, seldom prevails against greed, money or positional power. But I would add to this an opinion that sometimes the exercise of power is almost innocent, or, if not innocent, accidental. .

THE RANDOM HOUSE NEGOTIATION

One of the biggest opportunities to do something useful for the people of Carroll County came early in my legislative career. You have to understand that, while I was a major player in the action, a lot of other people can and will also claim credit. The truth is that when a major corporation moves into a community it has a major impact on jobs, incomes and the entire future of the impacted area. It is not surprising that people jump on the bandwagon and play a lot of music on the trip down the road. But you must remember that negotiations are seldom held in public and there are always hidden stories to tell. Well, here is one about the Random House deal.

It started in 1963, a few days after I arrived in Annapolis as a newly elected member of the Legislature. On that day, I was sitting by myself at a table in the basement lunch room of the State House when a lady approached and asked if she could share the table.

"I'm Renee Goff." She said. "I'm the special assistant to Governor Tawes' wife." She settled down and we ate in silence for a moment, then she put down her fork and addressed me directly. "Delegate Yingling, I'm aware that you work for a publishing house. I wonder if you can help me with a project."

"What's that?" I asked. I have to admit that I was a bit startled to find that anyone in the Governor's Office even knew I was alive, let alone what I did for a living. At that stage I had a lot to learn about networking and how governments actually work.

"Mrs. Tawes has written a cookbook. We want to get it published professionally. Can you help us do that?"

"Well, I'm not really sure. I work for the L. W. Singer Division of Random House. This is the Textbook Division and we don't handle cookbooks. But I can talk to my boss and see what he can suggest." She didn't tell me at that moment that they had already approached a number of other publishers unsuccessfully.

I did call my boss and he referred the question upstairs to his boss. Somewhat to my surprise, shortly thereafter, the Editor in Chief appeared on the scene. After reviewing the material, he agreed to publish Mrs. Tawes' cookbook. To this point in time, all I had done was make one phone call.

Mrs. Tawes let me know that she and the Governor were both appreciative of my help. She was the love of his life and , as things turned out, he would do almost anything for someone who had helped her.

Random House in those days functioned very well and the editorial people involved in processing Mrs. Tawes' book kept me well informed of its progress through the system. During peripheral conversations about the cookbook, I learned that Random House was interested in building distribution center somewhere in Pennsylvania or Maryland. When I heard the news, the search was well along. Mister Richard Kislick, who was responsible for implementing the search, favored a place in Pennsylvania although I discovered that they had looked at several locations in Maryland.

In conversations with the Governor, I suggested that perhaps he should use his good offices to help insure that Random House would pick Maryland as the site. I knew, at that moment, that Mister Kislick had looked at a site in Carroll County, but that, at this point in time, it was not their first choice.

"Jake, what is it you feel I can do to help them decide on Maryland?"

"I suspect, Sir, that it might help if you were to call Bennett Cerf and tell him of your personal interest." I understand that he loves the water. Would it be possible to invite him down to spend a day on the yacht? That would give you a chance to get to know him, and at the same time tell him what a great and wonderful state Maryland is."

"Jake, will you go ahead and invite him down?"

"Well, Governor, a call from your office would have more impact."

"Tell you what. You make the call. You invite him down. I'll make the yacht available to you whenever you need it. You can make up the guest list."

I called Bennett Cerf's office and pointed out that since Mister Cert was aware that he was publishing Mrs. Tawes' cookbook, he might like to come down and be the Governor's guest on the state yacht for a day.

"It will be a day of good food and good company on the water." I said as persuasively as I could. A bit to my surprise, Bennett Cerf immediately accepted the invitation. Naturally, I had made it very clear that my call represented the Governor's personal invitation.

I immediately went ahead with the invitation list. Since we were textbook publishers, I took the opportunity to include some people who provide helpful conversation about educational areas. My key invitee was Doctor Pullen, the State Superintendent of Schools.

"Doctor Pullen," I asked. Would you like to spend a day on the Governor's yacht?"

"I've never been on that boat the entire time I've been School Superintendent."

"Yes, Sir. I can understand that. But I'm inviting you now."

"How do you get to do that?"

I explained as carefully as I could that the yacht was mine for a day and I'd been told I could invite anybody I wished. He accepted. Then, I called Chuck Ecker because he was an old friend of mine, and a school administrator in the state. Chuck subsequently became Howard County Executive. I also invited Dick Bobbitt who was my immediate boss at Singer. The finalized list included Governor and Mrs. Tawes, Mister and Mrs. Cerf, Doctor Pullen, Dick Bobbitt, Chuck Ecker and me.

With that in hand, I made the other arrangements. The Cerfs were to come down the night before and stay as the Governor's guests at Government House. I was loaned the Governor's limousine, complete with driver, so I could pick up the Cerfs at the airport and deliver them to their quarters. Then, at my own expense, I laid on a party for that evening. This was designed to let the Cerfts meet a number of the big guns in the state.

These included the Governor and his wife, Mayor McKeldin of Baltimore and his wife, Renee Goff, O'Dell Smith, the Governor's speech writer, my wife Genny, and the Governor's brother. Additionally, the group included George Hubley, Director of Economic Development for the state.

When the Cerfs' flight arrived at the airport, I rode out to the plane in the limousine and greeted them. Naturally, this had all been cleared for me in advance by the Governor's staff. My position in this was shaky at best. I was a very junior legislator and a Republican in a Democratic Administration to boot. I wasn't an old line Democrat. I was just a minor league textbook salesman working for a subsidiary of Random House. Bennet Cerf, himself, had probably never heard of me. I've never been sure he even knew I worked for him. You have to put the whole thing down to that fine old word I heard so often in the legislature. It was pure 'chutzpah'.

The party came off perfectly as did the next day which was spent on the boat. Everybody relaxed and let their hair down. McKeldin and Tawes were gracious and friendly with each other although occupying diametrically opposite poles in the political spectrum. Both men thoroughly enjoyed the other's political war stories.

The next day, as we proceeded down the Bay, the Governor, Bennett Cerf and I ended up sitting on the fan tail. While walking back to the stern with them, I had tried to explain my discomfort at being caught between two such powerful men, but I didn't exactly succeed.

"Governor," I said. "I'm just a bottom of the rung salesman in one of Mister Cerf's companies. I have no real influence in Random House. In fact, I doubt that Mister Cerf even known really knows me."

"Well, Jake, that may all be true, but it looks to me as though you're moving things right along."

"Sir, why don't you just sort of let me slip into the background so you two can talk face to face."

"No, no. You just sit right over there with us." At that point, Bennett Cerf, who had half heard the conversation, chipped in.

"That's right, Jake. You just sit right down in the middle."

So I ended up sitting between the Governor and Bennett Cerf on the fantail bench. The two of them talked right over, under and around me until Governor Tawes decided to cut to the chaff. He paused for a moment then switched off the nitty-gritty and got to the meat.

"Bennett," he said. "We want you to put your new distribution center in Maryland. In fact, I understand Jake thinks you should locate in Carroll County. Well, I want you both to know that would be just fine with me." I became very nervous at this point and hastened to add a moderating remark.

"In Maryland, Governor. I'd love to have Random House come to Carroll County, but the most important thing to me is that they come to Maryland." The Governor just laughed.

"Jake's young at this business, but he's for sure a politician. Bennett, whatever it is you want, whatever it is you need, you just tell Jake and it will be there for you."

He really said 'tell Jake'. He didn't say tell my office. He said 'tell Jake what you need'. Well, hell, I didn't believe for one minute that Bennett Cerf was going to tell me anything. But that was exactly the way it turned out. The Governor said it again. "You tell Jake what you need, because we want you to come down here."

Parenthetically, it should be noted that on this evening my near teetotaler style was greatly rewarded. As the Governor and Mister Cerf enjoyed their libations and the ocean breezes, I settled back on the bench and spoke only when spoken to. The Ship of State was steering itself right into Carroll County and I carefully and gravely avoided its wake.

Bennett and Mrs. Cerf blew back to New York feeling good about the visit and I went hack to work. It was just a short time later when Richard Kislik called me and said he'd been instructed to take a good look at Carroll County. At this point, rumors were running all over Annapolis and some of them reached home. Scott Bair, a local mover and shaker, called me.

"I understand Random House is looking for a place in Maryland. Is that right?"

"Yes. That's my understanding also."

"Well, Jake, I'd like to see them place that installation in Carroll County. In fact, I have an option on a perfect piece of property near to town but out far enough to not impact traffic downtown. It is close to 140 for trucking."

I understood that this piece of property was already under consideration by Kislik. I told Scott Bair this immediately. Then, I added one caution.

"Well, I'll tell you what, Scott. You have to understand my position. I can't really discuss any particular piece of property at this time."

"I do understand that, but I want to tell you that if they're interested, I do hold an option on that land. I'll make it available if they're interested.'

What I took from that conversation was 'no cut for him' was implicit if Random House settled on that piece of property. So things had begun developing.

Random House did decide this property was worthy of consideration. People, including Bennett Cerf, came to town. They asked for advice on which local attorney to use. I recommended Earl Shipley. He drew up working papers for them.

Then, it turned out that the Industrial Revenue Bond enabling legislation needed modification. Bennett asked if I could handle that. I talked this over with the Governor and pointed out that, as a Republican Delegate, I lacked sufficient clout to push through the needed amendment. However, I stated that Senator Weant had that clout.

The Governor spoke with Weant and the Senator introduced and shepherded the bill to passage as 'emergency legislation'. This allowed the New York Bond Counsel to put together a deal which qualified Carroll County to receive industrial revenue bonds. Carroll County became the first county to use industrial revenue bonds that way.

Somewhere along the line, Scott Bair said he needed to talk with Bennett Cerf personally, so I set up a luncheon. This included Scott and Bennett plus all three County Commissioners along with my boss, Dick Bobbitt. We all went over to what is now Cockey's Tavern but then was 'Miss Hoffman's'.

Thelma Hoffman ran the place with the restaurant downstairs and lodging upstairs. I called her up and asked for a corner table.

"Jake," she asked. "What's that for?" I told her. She was thrilled to hear Scott Bair was going to be there. For whatever reason she catered to Scott.

"Look, Thelma. I'll tell you, but you have to keep this quiet. We don't want to have to deal with reporters." Thelma agreed, but when we were all settled in she came over to the table and fawned all over Bennett Cerf.

"Oh, my God," she exclaimed. "It's Bennett Cerf from 'What's My Line." Bennett flattered her right back and that made her day, if not the entire month.

As a result of that meeting, Scott gave up the option. There were many meetings after that one, mostly attorney kind of things. I missed most of them. I explained my absence without apologies. I was being paid to spend my days selling textbooks, not acting like a legislator.

The one set of meetings I had to be around for happened when the Governor came to town to meet with Bennett. I was asked into these meetings from time to time. From this, some people gathered that I was the pusher, the guy with influence, the 'man' who had people's ears. I really didn't understand then how important a role I played. I, in fact, was a kind of buffer who could hear both sides without jeopardizing anyone. I was genuinely awed. I was, at best, a 33 year old junior and inexperienced legislator. This was my first real look at how power plays take place and deals are made.

For example, I sat in on a discussion of how the plant was going to be aligned on the property. There was a question of moving Hahn Road to accommodate the main entrance to the plant. An engineer for the State Roads Commission stated that there was no way the road could be changed. The Governor let the conversation run its course, then he turned to directly face Bennett Cerf.

"Bennett, it seems we're not going to be able to settle this problem this afternoon, but I assure you that tomorrow morning there will be someone sitting in that chair who will make that change happen."

All of a sudden that negatively disposed Engineer decided he'd been wrong. There was a way that road could and should be moved. And it subsequently was.

George Grier, a Carroll County man of all parts, was the present Executive Assistant to the Commissioners.. He played a role in all these meetings. He made at least two trips to New York. He handled all of the needed permits and supervised most of the technical details of the deal. He was the cog who kept the wheels greased and moving. To the extent that everything runs on detail, George became the key man in making the deal real.

Ultimately, a couple of years down the pike, my deal making cost me my job with L. W. Singer. My boss evidently got his nose out of joint over my high level association with the Governor and with Bennett Cerf.

Dick Bobbitt was one of the sharpest, smoothest, most charismatic men I have known. But Dick was also very ambitious. Even when I first encountered him as s Sales Manager with L. W. Singer, he aspired to someday becoming President of Singer. He worked hard at that goal and toward becoming an officer of the parent company, Random House.

Unfortunately, one night when he stayed overnight at my house, he got deep into the scotch and said a lot of things that would best have been left unsaid. I believe that from that point on he felt threatened by my having such clear knowledge of his plans. I suspect he feared I might talk about them. In the summer of 1965 I received a telephone call from him.

"As of the first of next month, you are no longer with the Company."

"What are you saying?" I had gone into shock.

"You heard me! That's it! You have a lot of ability. You have a lot of skills, but your future is probably in government or politics, not in L. W. Singer."

I was shocked and deeply hurt. It might have been different if I had failed as a salesman, but I hadn't. Even with all of the legislative based distractions, I still had a first rate sales record. Well, be that as it may, my career as a textbook salesman was history. Within thirty days, I had a better job and was making more money.

I could have attended the Random House Distribution Center dedication. I certainly received an invitation. But I was bitter and declined. I was now working as a Sales Manager and could have made myself available. Bennett called me to ask why I had not been there.

"Bobbitt fired me." I said, without trying to disguise my anger.

"I wish I had known.." I appreciated Bennett's thought but we both knew the act could not be recalled. It was already water over the dam.

Even now, I can think back and laugh as I see myself getting out of the Governor's limousine and greeting Bennett and his wife. Here was this little ol' country boy from Carroll County acting like running around in the Governor's limousine with a State Trooper escort was the most natural thing in the world. Well, it may have been mostly bluff on my part, but it was a damn good bluff, if I say so myself.

**Governor Tawes, Jake, and Bennett Cerf on fantail of
'The Maryland Lady'**

**Governor signs bill enabling Random House
to build in Carroll County
Back: Wilbur Magin, Bill Dulaney, Jake Yingling, and
Tom O'Farrell
Seated: Marvin Mandel, Bill James, Gov. Tawes, Jim
Maus, the Chief Clerk**

MY SECOND RUN FOR OFFICE

Second time around, I had hands-on experience in the Legislature which I could point to. I had served on The Ways and Means Committee, The Education Committee, The Motor Vehicle Committee, the Alcoholic Beverages Committee, the Legislative Council Sub-Committee on Tourism, and also The Metropolitan Committee. I had also served as a member and Chairman for the Maryland World's Fair Speaker's Bureau.

I essentially repeated the promises I had made during my first run for office. **Four years ago when I was seeking election to the House of Delegates, I made a pledge to the people of Carroll County to always be available to them. During my time in office, I have kept that pledge. I feel it is just as timely today as it was four years ago. I therefore repeat it. (The only substantial changes were that my boys were now four years older.)**

THE LEGISLATURE GRINDS ON

Altogether, through three terms, I served ten years as a delegate to the legislature. As I understood more about how the legislature works and how my committees functioned, I expanded my activities to include the introduction of a number of bills and dealt with a number of controversial issues.

Among my own bills was one calling for the re-examination of motorists every five years. A related bill required the compulsory installation of seatbelts. I also made an effort to permit the deduction of college expenses from gross income. I supported horse racing legislation. I opposed many bills, one of which would have required that banks use attorneys whenever estates were adjudicated. I also opposed a bill proposing revision of the tax code. From the weighty to the almost insignificant, I opposed a bill which would have required barber shops to fix days and hours of work.

To give you an idea of how complex some bills can become, I originally sponsored a redistricting bill but was forced to oppose it when the final form, modified in session, proved damaging to the interests of Carroll County voters.

The one guarantee I can give you is that, during the legislative year, there was never any escape from turmoil, both internal and external.

This turmoil was not just limited to legislative matters. The entire nation seemed to be spinning in the late sixties. There were protests against U. S. policy in Vietnam. Israeli and Jordanian forces were battling in Hebron. The six day war between Israel and the Arabs flared up. Martin Luther King was assassinated in Memphis. Robert Kennedy was killed in Los Angeles. Amid all this, Richard Nixon was elected by the smallest majority since 1912.

This third time around I had even stronger legislative credentials to present to the electorate. I had already served in the House of Delegates for seven years. I had been a member of the Judiciary Committee as well as numerous subcommittees of the Legislative Council. I had been a member of the Planning Council and involved with the Governor's Study Group on Vocational Rehabilitation. My major campaign theme asked the votes to **Keep a strong, effective and respected voice for Carroll County in the State House.**

My extra curricular activities included: Board Director at St. Joseph's hospital in Towson; continued work with the Kiwanis Club: Director of the Westminster Trust Company; Director of Independent Liberty Life Insurance Company; and a membership on the Board of Visitors at the Maryland School for the Deaf. I also belonged to the American Society for Training and Development and was a member of the National Committee for Support of Public Schools.

There were times in the mid-sixties when I felt as though I was living in a huge wind tunnel. Initially, as a young book man (traveler in the publisher's vernacular) I regularly visited all of the public and private schools in Washington, D.C. In the mid-fifties I'd felt totally safe. All that changed in the Sixties. I don't know that I can blame this on Brown versus the Board of Education, but its decision seemed to trigger an attitudinal change of some sort. The schools were now integrated but some were still called 'black schools'. Areas where, formerly, I had felt perfectly safe were now experiencing high crime rates. Racial tensions now prevailed in most of my metropolitan work areas.

In fact, several school system administrators suggested that I needed to have a guard accompany me to the classrooms of the department heads I wished to visit. I no longer felt safe, not even in the hallways of some schools. I suspect this is one reason I accepted Dick Bobbitt's infamous decree without a more flamboyant response.

More of my legislative adventures, along with newspaper accounts of some, are documented in the after notes. For now, let me turn to a brief recounting of my days as a training and educational consultant.

The change in roles was probably not even noticed by my colleagues in the House of Delegates, nor did it seem to be of any interest to my legislative constituents in Carroll County. Although I did considerably broader traveling in my new role, I was still able to meet and greet the voters when required.

In many ways the work was very much the same but the clients were much more varied and the problems were directed toward helping communities procure training grants rather than supplying schools with textbooks.

WESTINGHOUSE LEARNING

This firm was a division of the Westinghouse Corporation. Westinghouse Learning had been established in response to many of the dictates of President Johnson's Great Society. Its formation represented Westinghouse's corporate commitment to devising and managing programs designed to help specific urban communities. Note that word 'urban'. This Company was formed to go directly into the kinds of situation I had watched develop in the District of Columbia. One reason I was hired was because I had personally experienced the 'urban condition' concerning Mister Johnson and the management of Westinghouse.

I started out with the Learning Corporation in their national sales department. My job involved traveling to many of the major cities in the U.S., assessing their needs, and determining how available federal funded grants could help make the individual communities function better.

One of my first jobs was as part of a team assigned to assess the Pittsburgh Police Department with an eye as to how they could better serve their various and diversified communities. To help study the problem, I was assigned to ride as an observer in patrol cars. In order to preserve the integrity and confidentiality of the study, even the Duty Sergeants were not told who I was or why I was there.

The Assistant Police Commissioner with whom we worked notified each Precinct that I was to accompany chosen policemen on their rounds. It was made clear that the patrol officers were not responsible for my safety and that I was to be considered capable of taking care of myself.

Unfortunately, there was a pattern which repeated every time I climbed into a squad car. The senior man in the team wanted to know who I was and what I was doing there. In all cases I had been instructed that his questions could be answered only by his superiors at the precinct level.. Naturally, that set up an attitude of suspicion. Was I there to help them or was I there to spy on them? This, definitely, was a design flaw in the study.

In spite of the system imposed difficulties, I did get involved in may interesting examples of exactly how the Pittsburgh Policemen acted and reacted within their own environments. Then, our internal staff was able to devise training programs which would effectively improve both police performance and acceptability by the people with whom they interacted. Naturally, a lot of this work could be dismissed as just 'common sense', but that's not how policemen are normally trained to react. There are safety and public relations issues they must face every day that 'just common sense' will not normally address.

For example, in one case I watched with interest, our car received a report from the precinct that a father had reported that his daughter had been raped. He said he knew the man who had done the deed. "I want the bastard arrested!"

Our Squad Leader got the accused man's name and address. We drove to his home, wrested him from bed, handcuffed him while still in his pajamas, then took him down to the Station House.

The father and the daughter were summoned to the Station House. When they arrived, the detectives questioning the boy already had his story. He was in love with the girl. She was in love with him. They'd had sex alright but it was not rape. They were of age and the sex was consensual. The boy didn't understand why he'd been pulled from his bed.

The same detectives interviewed the girl. She said she too was in love. The sex, she agreed, was consensual. It was just that her father had intercepted her when she arrived home late. She'd appeared disheveled and had been afraid to tell her father about having sex. She'd lied and cried rape.

It seemed obvious that taking the boy into custody had been hasty. Had the boy been questioned first, enough suspicion of the charge would have existed to justify the detectives being called on to question the girl before the boy was taken into custody. The bad conditions created all around could have been prevented.. As it was, the boy's parents were furious at the girl's father. Any possibility of 'love conquering all' had vanished.

In another example, I found myself at risk because of the secrecy with which our survey was being conducted. The senior officer in my assigned squad car received a radio call which reported a possible warehouse break-in. The two police officers got out to approach the front door. The senior officer, not realizing I was not a police officer, merely a civilian on a ride-along supervisory exercise, suggested I cover the back door. I was, of course, not armed. You have no idea how relieved I was when they wandered back in a few minutes and told me it had been a false alarm.

We wrote our report and got out of Pittsburgh. I was immediately ordered to another research task in another town. This was another systemic flaw. The people who conducted the initial study and wrote the report were never briefed on the ultimate results. Was a program funded? Had our findings been found valid? I didn't know then and I don't know now. I just found the entire experience both harassing and exciting.

One of my assignments in Pittsburgh was not with the Police but with the black community, mostly in sections between downtown and the Oakland area surrounding the University of Pittsburgh as well as on the lower Northside which lay just over the river from downtown.

Our assignment was to gather information about attitudes and living conditions in the black communities.

In truth, everyone felt it was just not safe for a white man to pursue this study on his own. Therefore, I was assigned a bodyguard, a gentleman named John Henry Johnson. John Henry had played fullback for the Pittsburgh Steelers. He was well known to be someone nobody in his right mind would mess with.

I learned to love John Henry immediately. We drove into the heart of one area in his old Cadillac and parked in front of a bar on a side street.

"I have to take a leak," said John Henry "G'wan in. I'll be right there."

Naively, I walked into the bar and nonchalantly ordered a beer.

"We don't serve honkeys." announced the bartender

"Yeah, Honkey, what the hell you doin' here? Maybe you better get yo ass outa here while yo still got it!" I turned to stare at the two black men who, obviously, didn't consider me worth a fart in a windstorm.

"I'm here with a friend." I said, not quite willing to follow my instincts, which were to get off that stood and run.

"You ain't got no friends in this place!" Just then John Henry appeared. He took one look, sized up the situation, and asked very quietly.

"Just what in the hell is going on here?"

"We gonna throw that smart mouthed honkey out the fuckin' door."

"Well, now. That's gonna be a trip. Mister Yingling is a friend of mine. If you hurt him, you hurt me!" You didn't need a refrigerator to chill the beer in that bar after that remark.

"John Henry, if that man's a friend of yours, he's sure as all hell a friend of ours."

After that, the word spread. I was a friend of John Henry Johnson's. Don't mess with Mister Yingling. I didn't have a minute's trouble after that. In retrospect, I'm not sure John Henry didn't set up the situation just to get the word out. Whatever, it sure worked.

From then on, I never had any trouble. John Henry had some sort of a PR job at Columbia Gas. He went in every morning, read the paper, then picked me up and escorted me around Pittsburgh. When John Henry was busy with his regular job, there was a five by five gentleman who'd played the line for the Cleveland Browns 'in the old days'. He wasn't as tall as John Henry but he was just as wide as he was high and it all seemed to be muscle. He, too, was always greeted with what I came to see as 'reverential respect' by the black community.

After a number of other hair-raising adventures in place such as Greenville, Mississippi, I was promoted to Supervisor of Project Administration. I had a staff reporting to me who were responsible for auditing our progress both inside the United States and abroad. We didn't have much going on outside the country, but I was slated to personally audit our program in Vietnam. I was about to leave when the Tet Offensive blew up the deal. That could have turned out worse than the snake pit I wandered into in East St. Louis, Missouri.

We had a community activist program in East St. Louis. It turned slightly hairy. This, in part, was due to the town having a white mayor while the largest growth area was the black community. I well remember one evening meeting when some of the community activists suggested out loud that if the Mayor didn't change some of his thinking, they just might have to remove him from office. And it seemed perfectly evident they didn't mean by way of the ballot box. A vote was taken that night and a Nun in the audience poured oil on the fire by encouraging the crowd to vote to take action "unless the 'most urgent' grievances are 'immediately' addressed by the Mayor".

Things became so bad that our man on the scene, our program director, a fellow named 'Chalker', was physically threatened to the point where we had to hire black guards to sneak him out of East St. Louis and hide him in a safe house. I remember Chalker partly because his birthday was September 30, the same as mine.

I never felt personally threatened by the evident militancy among that black community. My driver was one of their leaders. The fact was that my driver always had a loaded 38 on the seat beside him. Some local cops assured me that I was safer with him than I would have been with them. Then, too, one of the local leaders of The Black Panthers was completely sold on what we were trying to accomplish. That helped tremendously.

Despite my feeling safe, I almost lost my life in East St. Louis. On one of my last visits, I was departing for the airport when an unfortunate incident happened. I was sitting in the front seat of a car with a black driver. An employee of ours, a gal named Caroline was in back. A shot rang out. A bullet hit the right front door, ricocheted down through the glass and came out right at my feet. It came just inches away from taking me out. I heard later that the shot had all been a big mistake. The shooter thought I was somebody else.

At that same time, Westinghouse Learning also had programs running in New Mexico. I visited them on many occasions. It was on one of these trips that I met Ben Raskob.

Unlike East St. Louis, the people in Albuquerque and Santa Fe were very kind and very helpful. The key difference lay in the extra supportive attitudes of certain high placed officials. Among these was one highly placed man from the office of Governor David Cargo.

This was Johnny Jasper. Mister Jasper was highly regarded and ultimately was offered a position in the Nixon administration which he turned down.

Dr, Jerome Noskin was a community leader and chairman of the state republican party. I was fortunate to be invited to his house where we spent several hours discussing state, federal and international politics. Later, I was honored with a plaque presented by Governor Cargo. This declared me to be a New Mexico Colonel, an aide-de-camp to the Governor of the State of New Mexico.

Unlike being pursued by a bullet in East St. Louis, my only contretemps in New Mexico was with a female clerk in the car rental agency at the airport. She kept on suggesting we have a cup of coffee or something stronger sometime. Since she was more than just insistent, I became nervous about just picking up the car.

Finally, I arrived in Albuquerque in the company of Doctor Sarah Austin, a black lady who also worked for Westinghouse. She was heading for a different office in a separate part of town, but I asked her to hold on for a minute. I had seen the agency clerk giving me the usual big welcoming smile.

"Sarah, will you do me a real favor?" I asked. "Will you just walk over to the car rental counter with me? I need to nip a situation in the bud." Sarah agreed, so I walked on over and signed for the car. With that done, the girl smiled even more widely and announced.

"I'm off duty in five minutes. You car's being brought around. I'll see you outside."

Sarah and I walked outside and waited. As the young lady approached us, I turned to Sarah and asked loudly, "Honey, did you get all of your luggage?"

The rental clerk stopped dead in her tracks. She turned on her heel and stalked away. Never again did she invite me to share anything with her.

**PART FIVE:
BANKING,
INVESTING, AND
BOARD SERVICE**

BANKING, INVESTING AND BOARD SERVICE

I have already spoken about how my work and political lives intertwined. The third facet of my daily interests was in the useful employment of whatever funds came into my hands. Early on, I learned it was better to be able to pay my bills, then not. In fact, I learned not to incur bills when I was not sure as to how they were to be paid.

As a ten year old child, if I got as much as ten cents in my grubby little hands, I took it down to the First National Bank in Gettysburg and deposited it in my savings account. Today, if you tried to place ten cents in a bank, they would refuse it. They couldn't afford to process the transaction. But, even as late as 1940, with what was to become the war economy not yet booming, almost any amount was accepted.

I learned the value of consistent saving from that bank. Unfortunately, I also learned one other lesson. Just because people are in positions of trust does not mean they are trustworthy. One day as I stepped up to the cage of what I believed to be a totally trustworthy bank to make a deposit, I saw a five dollar bill at my feet. Even though there was no one who could have seen me pick it up, I asked the teller if anyone had reported that they had lost some money.

"Why?" he asked.

"Because I just found five dollars."

"Give it to me." he said without a moment's hesitation. "If anyone comes in and asks about it, I will give it to them"

A week later I approached that same teller and asked him about the five dollars. For some reason, he couldn't recall my giving it to him. To this day, I'm convinced he pocketed the money. That five dollars was a big deal to me, but there was no way to prove my case so I had to let go of it. If someone had claimed the money, I would have felt good about turning it in. On the other hand, having the teller keep it seemed to me to be nothing short of out and out theft. Later, that man became a respected banker, but to me he remained suspect and not trustworthy. I continued to believe that no one in those days could lose as much as five dollars and not be aware of it.

When I first decided to buy stock, it was in a bank, but in the Gettysburg Bank, not in First National. I can't say the two events were exactly consciously connected, but, on some level, I'm sure they were.

That first stock purchase came about just after we had moved to Westminster. It happened because when I was back in Gettysburg visiting a friend, he told me that Gettysburg National Bank had shares of stock for sale and that it might be a good deal for me. At that moment, I had just received a bonus and was looking for somewhere to invest the money. I also thought it might be ironic to buy stock in a Gettysburg Bank after having just moved from the town.

At the Gettysburg Bank, I asked the receptionist who I should see about buying stock in the bank. In a short time, Mister Wills, then Chairman of the Board, appeared and invited me into his office. He was a courtly gentleman and very curious as to why I wanted to buy stock in the bank.

"Who are you, Mister Yingling? Do I know your father?"

"I don't think so, Sir. But we all lived on South Washington Street in the Third Ward for over twenty years. " I went on to explain that I had attended the Catholic Elementary School, as well as Gettysburg High School and College. "Now, I live in Westminster, Maryland."

"Well, that's not real far off. Why did you move out of Gettysburg?"

"Well, Sir. It's because I just took a new job selling textbooks and it requires me to live in my territory." I hesitated for a moment, then explained further;. "In truth, there didn't seem to be much opportunity for me in Gettysburg because I just didn't have the right connections. I couldn't even get a job teaching here so I felt I could better myself by getting away from my roots."

"That's kind of a shame, but I can't blame you for moving under those conditions. Now, listen. There isn't really any bank stock available just now, but I like you. You seem like a nice young man. I'll sell you one hundred shares of my own personal stock."

So that's how my first stock purchase came to be 100 shares in the Gettysburg National Bank. A friend gave me bad information and a fine old gentleman took pity on a semi-ignorant young man who had no idea of how to buy stock.

I guess that's another lesson. Any time I've had money to buy something, somebody turned up to sell it to me. This became increasingly true for me during the Seventies. During those years I made a reasonable number of stock purchases but they mostly were through personal connections, not through bankers. I knew the people, the institutions and the situations I invested in through first hand contact.

In those years I was very active in the Westminster Community. My participation in local life actually began in 1962 when I became President of the Westminster Kiwanis Club. At thirty-two, I was the youngest president the club had ever had. There were a lot of influential people in the Kiwanis Club and many of them showed me great kindness. I was received in Westminster in a way a boy from the Third Ward never would have been received in Gettysburg.

One member of Kiwanis was Paul Kuhns. At that time, Mister Kuhns was the Executive Vice President of Westmisnter Bank and

Trust Company. Eventually, he asked me if I would consider becoming a member of their board. Prior to this, I had already begun investing money in Westminster Bank and Trust Company.

I became a member of that board. Today, there is a bronze plaque inside the bank's primary office on Main Street in Westminster which lists that Board of Directors. I am the only living director whose name shows on that plaque. During my early years on the Board I accumulated additional stock. By 1971, I was tied, or perhaps alone, as the second largest shareholder in the bank. In 1971 we were purchased by Mercantile Bank and stock, which I still own, multiplied many times.

Simultaneously, I acquired shares in Union National Bank. As of today, I am one of the largest individual shareholders in Union National Bank.

In 1983 I was advised that a large block of Taneytown Bank and Trust Company was for sale. I managed to purchase those shares , then later, achieved two other purchases. In 1986, Carroll Meyers, who had been a friend for years, and the President of Taneytown Bank and Trust, suggested that I come on their Board. I resigned from the Board of Westminster Bank and Trust Company and did so.

After selling some shares in Taneytown Bank and Trust, the shares I retained became shares in F&M Bank. These remaining shares are now worth more than what I paid for the original investment in Taneytown.

I've gone into the details of these bank investments because my financial success has raised questions in some people's minds as to where my money came from. People seem to always suspect people who have been active in politics or have held government jobs. Although I feel that my financial status is no one's concern except mine, I want it known that I can document fully every investment, and every asset I still own. None of my money came from being a member of the legislature or from being a state government employee. I invested in people and companies that l understood inside and out. I watched my investments with an eagle eye. I happily and gratefully paid every cent of taxes that I've owed.

One other investment I do want to detail came about as a result of my membership in the Kiwanis Club. While active in Kiwanis, I became friends with Frank Libman. At that time Frank and four other men were on the Board of Westminster Hardware Company. One of the Board members retired and asked the other members if they would accept me on the Board if he sold me his shares. They agreed. The members of the Board, in addition to Frank Libman, were Walter Haines who owned a dry cleaning business; Dave Babylon who was a director of Carroll County Bank and a prominent local business man; and Mister Stoner, who was one of the owners of Westminster

Nurseries. With the purchase of the retiring board member's shares I became the largest shareholder in Westminster Hardware

As other principals died off, their estates decided to sell their shares. The Board discussed the opportunity to purchase more shares personally. Mister Haines and Mister Stoner decided not to increase their holdings. Mister Babylon said: "You two guys are the active ones now. I'll sell you my stock." At that point, Frank Libman and I ended up with 95% of. Westminster Hardware.

The primary assets consisted of real estate on Main Street and John Street. Frank and I then negotiated the purchase of the old Southern States building where we started a division called Plumbing, Heating and Supplies. Frank and I decided to liquidate the company in 1986. Again, the money received from this investment was re-invested in other ventures.

A Cautionary Note About Serving On Boards

Many of my friends who have never been invited to serve on a Board of Directors feel that Board membership is purely an unearned perk. They are unaware of the legal, financial and moral jeopardy such membership can pose. They are unaware of the conflicts which can develop among board members and organizational management. I was invited to serve on my first bank board in 1962 at age 32. This was the Westminster Trust Company.

I was young for the job, but I had met Paul Kuhns, who issued the invitation, in Kiwanis. Paul was aware of the work within Kiwanis which had led to my being elected President. Secondly, I was serving in the Legislature. Thirdly, I had launched a program to gradually accumulate a strong stock position in the bank company.

At that time, Westminster Trust had no formal training program for newly appointed or elected people, but I found other board members to be willing and able guides and mentors. Later, I served on a number of other bank boards as well as on the boards of several not-for-profit organizations.

The first lesson I learned is that the Directors are responsible for the management of the business or not-for-profit organization. The directors are responsible to the shareholders or membership. In a business organization the shareholders may remove the directors from office. In both cases, the board member has an obligation to reveal any possible conflicts of interest and to behave diligently and prudently. He is bound not to use his position for personal gain. This covers any information he is privy to as a board member.

As I became a more experienced Board Member, I found many examples of conflicts of interest among both directors and organizational managers. Fully exercising a director's responsibility often proved difficult, and on occasion, impossible.

I have been in situations where a director's insistence on receiving the detailed information from management that is required for good decision making was considered to be 'micro-management' of the organization's work effort. In other words the need for information is seen as interference with management's right to manage the enterprise. Since I have always insisted on proceeding in an absolutely straight line and never cutting any questionable deals, I usually prevailed n my efforts to offer a contribution, On a few occasions, I was forced to resign from a Board in order to preserve my own integrity. Similar situations occurred in both for-profit and not-for-profit organizations.

Boards of Directors of organizations which, on the surface, should be totally ethical, frequently are not.

No matter how great the desire to protect certain individuals, the Board members must face up to evident problems. There is no hiding from them. Believe me I had to learn how to ask deeper and more penetrating questions. especially when funding was at stake. If that was true for me when acting as a consultant, it was doubly true for me as a board member.

Beyond this, I continue to feel that Boards must operate at arms length with key managers. Their duties and goals are sufficiently different that they need to act almost independently.

PART SIX:

POLITICS AS I EXPERIENCED IT
MORE ABOUT MY LEGISLATIVE YEARS
MY OWN PERSONAL 'WHAT IF?'
OTHER ANNAPOLIS YEARS
SHELTERED HOUSING
OTHER POLITICAL PEOPLE AND PLACES
WHAT DOES IT ALL ADD UP TO?

POLITICS AS I EXPERIENCED IT

I was active in politics and state government from 1962 through 1979, and an active observer both before and after that time, right up till today in fact. I still maintain many of my legislative contacts and am in almost constant contact with a variety of political activists on all levels. To those of us who played it for an extended period of time, politics is the greatest game ever invented.

Every day offers a crisis and a reward. Every day you ride the wind, watch a volcano blow or feel the tremors from a genuine earthquake. It can be the greatest ego boosting and ego destroying experience anyone can go through. People love you. People hate you. And you're not always sure which is which.

There are three essentials for anyone who chooses to play the game and run for office.

The first of these is achieving an understanding of how you can get elected in your own community if that's where you wish to serve. Going for a State office is more complicated. Going for Federal office requires much more money and much broader support.

The second essential is learning to achieve competency in the duties of the office to which you are first elected, then becoming competent in any other offices to which you succeed or are appointed..

The third essential is learning to 'network'. You have to learn who does what well. Where can you go to find facts you can trust? Who can you trust to give you an honest appraisal.? Who can help shape your attitudes on any of a thousand potential topics with which you must contend creatively and honestly?

Meeting and greeting and remembering faces is very important. When serving in the legislature, you must remember and manage an astonishing amount of detail about a wide ranging series of issues. On any given day, you can be faced with bills or discussions concerning everything from banking mergers up to crop and livestock management as well as highway and mass transit issues. You are constantly assaulted by health care, drug, education and aging problems shouting for attention and solutions. You quickly find there is no issue without partisans.

Above all, you have to have firmed up a good understanding of your constituents' beliefs about their rights, privileges and duties. While you can take a disparate stand on an occasional issue, mostly you must reflect the mores and morals of your community.

Carroll County, Maryland, at the time of my first election, was firmly Democratic although ultra conservative. In time that changed to be expressed by a switch to become more a Republican stronghold. It was and is a farm community with mostly Christian beliefs.

Traditional inner city conflicts were initially minor issues in its basically rural towns. There was an existing 'old boys network' but it was not as crusty or implacable toward outsiders as you may find in strongly adhesive (ethnic or religiously intolerant areas) city areas. At the time of my first election there were relatively few movers and shakers and they were easier to meet than similar individuals in more urban areas.

In fact, Carroll County old family names were almost identical with the names found in Gettysburg, Pennsylvania. Indeed, many of the families were interrelated. Mostly, many of us shared a common Germanic heritage. Many of our ancestors had been refugees from the Palatine (Rhine Valley) based wars.

Even the town-gown division was similar. Just as Gettysburg College people tended to hold themselves slightly aloof from the community, so did the faculty and staff of Western Maryland College. Nowadays the dichotomy seems to have lessened but in those days it was notable. Perhaps it was merely that local involvement was less rewarding to the academics than participation in activities which brought good reviews from contemporaries in their own academic fields. This is not a criticism, merely a perception.

But all of that aside, being named 'Yingling' in a county accustom to the name was much better than running for office in a county to whom 'Junglin'' or 'Juengling', or any of a dozen other variants would have seemed strangely foreign, and not native. In short, whereas my phonically pronounced German name might have been a problem in an Irish or Swedish community, in Carroll County it was accepted as normal.

Above all, and I never kidded myself about this, in those days the legislative job did not pay much. It was regarded as a part time job, not the source of a livable income. I could afford it because it fit in with the type of work I was doing. Had I held a normal, eight to five type job, I never could have afforded the run or the subsequent service.

MORE ABOUT MY LEGISLATIVE YEARS

In my second legislative terms, my efforts were directed at improving our state educational opportunities, improving conditions for hired employees of volunteer fire departments, and supporting the development of a community college in Carroll County, opposing increases in county tax rates, supporting tax relief for farm items, and supporting the development of a strong league of women voters branch in Carroll County. I proposed a bus flashing lights law as the result of a child's death in the county.

My proposal for a strong conflict of interest law led to conflict. On several occasions I tangled with commissioners on issues such as the proper construction of a new county jail. I felt the proposed plan was inadequate to serve the public properly in future years.

My legislative record is heavily and highly documented. What is not always evident is the climate within which the legislature worked. Many of our meetings spent more time on outside happenings than on the actual bills under discussion. Among the heavily impacting items was the election of Spiro T. Agnew to the office of Governor in 1967. Then, he resigned to become Vice President of the United States. He was followed in office by Marvin Mandel in 1969. In 1973 Agnew resigned the Vice Presidency and pleaded 'no contest' to a felony charge. Needless to say, all of these changes heavily impacted the work of the legislature.

From my point of view, Agnew had the makings of a good governor but he'd wandered into deep water when he became Nixon's VP. Unfortunately, the good things Agnew did for Maryland became submerged by the misery he encountered while in Washington. It had become apparent to me that Mandel's election by the legislature in 1969 had become inevitable. Agnew's problems had not yet surfaced and had no impact on Mandel's selection. Both houses of the legislature were heavily Democratic and I was sure this represented the will of the electorate. Beyond that, Marvin Mandel was speaker of the house and had demonstrated his great abilities to get legislation drawn and passed.

Marvin Mandel and I had previously discussed his run for Governor and whether I could support him. As I now recall, only three Republican members voted for Marvin on the first roll call. They were Loretta Nimmerrichter from Charles county, and Dick Mathews and me from Carroll County.

Loretta had indicated earlier that she'd support Marvin and Dick and I had discussed the situation at length. I indicated that a party line vote would ultimately not be to the best interests of Carroll County. There was no way Marvin's election could be stopped. It seemed to me that it was plainly in the interests of Carroll County that we support Marvin Mandel's election.

My vote came at the end of the roll call and was not needed to assure Marvin Mandel's election, but I had pledged my word to the Speaker and I kept it. Before the roll call, Marvin had called me aside to say that if he had enough votes in hand, he would understand if I voted for Rogers Morton. I replied that I had pledged my word and no matter what the situation, he would receive my vote.

I still have the official ballot recording the first vote taken. I am not sure anyone else preserved this ballot with its official count and pertinent signatures.

My official charge as a member of our legislative delegation was to work to the best interests of Carroll County. In this light, Democrat or not, I felt my supporting Marvin Mandel would ultimately work to the best interests of the County.

Earlier, I had taken another shot at correcting a systemic flaw in the way members of the Carroll County School Board were selected. Prior to 1967, members of the school board were chosen by the State Central Committee and submitted to the Governor for approval. The citizens of Carroll County had little, or no, say in the selection of the people who controlled their children's education.

I was mainly responsible for changing this system to one in which a committee of citizens was formed. People who wished to be elected to the Board could appear before the committee and indicate their qualifications. This committee then sent its recommendations to the Governor.. I partly defused the political nature of the preceding system. The newspapers were laudatory. One headline read "Mr. Yingling 's plan is Quite Clever".

"The selection of the Board members will still be made by the political party, assuming that the parties continue to make their selections in good faith, by a council made up of representatives from the various clubs in the County who will recommend the candidates to the party.

"First, it will weed out the phonies, those who aspire to the job while having no ability to fill it. Since each of the candidates will be subject to a question and answer period at a public meeting, the fakers should be easy to spot. Secondly, it will allow all citizens who are qualified and interested to be heard, whether or not they are active political workers."

It is truly said that any politically based change is never without opposition or detractors. I certainly experienced many of what can only be called 'attacks' during my legislative work.. I always tried to respond with moderate and modest enthusiasm. I was successful in most cases. However, I was not always permitted to reply with restraint. One example of such an adversarial public demonstration occurred in 1967.

In 1966 Scott Bair, Jr. was one of three Carroll County Commissioners, I leave it to the newspaper articles and the editorials of that time to evaluate the contributions he offered during his term of office. Mostly, I found these articles to be critical of him and to label his actions 'arrogant and obnoxious'. He opposed many of the suggestions made by hired outside experts which recommended things such as: the construction of a new jail; the building of new schools for a growing population; and many other forward looking proposals.

There was a meeting of the Regional Planning Council in 1967 at which I chaired a meeting during which a committee attempted to explain the workings of the Regional Planning Council to the citizens of Carroll County. In his own inimical style, Mister Bair brought a number of his supporters to join the over 200 other interested citizens who attended.

Bair's supporters harassed, heckled and challenged speakers all through the presentation. They had no idea of what the Regional Planning Council was all about nor did they want to hear any clarification. They arrived anti and departed without paying any heed to any of the positive matters we attempted to discuss. In short, we tried to point out that, even though Carroll County was not a part of any other jurisdiction such as Baltimore City or County, we could cooperate with them on projects offering actual benefits. This cooperation would have provided definite advantages to Carroll County.

Mister Bair's personal conduct at the meeting was referred to in a less than gracious manner by the attending press. Conversely, I received numerous letters from responsible citizens in the County complimenting me on the conduct of the meeting and how I was able to maintain my cool in the face of unreasoned adversity. I quote one letter from George Thomas, a former superintendent of schools.

"Mr. Yingling, I would like to compliment you on the restraint and gentlemanly conduct you displayed in your role during the Regional Planning Council (meeting) last Monday night, the 25th of June, 1967. You endured a situation designed to reduce you to a similar low level of irresponsible conduct, but you withstood the assault and performed in a manner always (calculated) to bring credit (to) yourself. It has been my misfortune to have been subjected before others, and in the press, to this same form of disgusting treatment (when it was) completely undeserved. I can understand your feelings and I'm sure y our determination to stand always for better objectives in a calm, determined and gentlemanly manner, continues.

Best Wishes, George E. Thomas"

I would hate to leave you with the impression that my time in the Legislature was all fuss and fury. Far from it! The daily contact with my colleagues was a sheer joy and. even when we opposed each other's bills, we worked to a common purpose with a finely honed sense of camaraderie.

Each year the Governor sponsored a Legislative Ball. This is held in Annapolis and is truly a grand affair. My first year, since there was no planned pre-ball party, I decided to throw one. I made arrangements at Carver Hall to provide food and drink for several hundred guests. I didn't think it was a big deal at the time and the cost was estimated to be less than one thousand dollars. In truth, it turned out to be a considerably bigger blast than I had imagined.

I sent a request to Republican members of the Florida State Legislature requesting that they send me some oranges because we were planning to serve a drink called **THE BIG ORANGE.** It really only had two ingredients: bourbon and orange juice. At that time, there were only four Republican House members and one Senator in the Florida Legislature. They were happy to get my request and responded with a few cases of oranges. In return, I promised to ship them Maryland oysters should they ever decide to have such an event.

I dispatched invitations to all the members of the Maryland Legislature and to appropriate State Officials. Everybody RSVP'd including every legislator and the Controller of the Treasury. Simultaneously, I invited the Governor. When I invited the Governor, he said he'd love to come, but he was entertaining the Admiral from the Naval Academy and a few other friends. He made a counter offer. If I could break away from my party for a time, perhaps I'd like to drop by his party. I was honored to do so.

As it turned out, I was the only Republican invited to join that small group. I think one reason I was invited was that I had invited Ted Service, the Chief Editor at L. W. Singer and a man who had been most helpful with Mrs. Tawes' cookbook to accompany me to the ball.

At an appropriate moment, I excused myself from my party and went over to join the Governor's party. It was a small party. There were less than a dozen couples. The Governor then suggested that I join their party as they entered the ballroom on the Naval Academy grounds. I was delighted to do so.

To the sound of 'Maryland, My Maryland' and with horses leading the way, we marched into the ballroom. Both Republican colleagues and Democratic influence makers wondered just what the hell Jake Yingling was doing marching in stride with the Governor and his party.

I don't believe my fellow legislators ever received an answer to the question even though some of them asked it right out loud. But you have to understand that this event set me up, good or bad, for future relationships with my colleagues on both sides of the aisle. My fellow Republicans, I suspect, were somewhat suspicious and the Democrats never figured out just how in the hell this could have happened for a freshman Republican legislator.

The morning after the ball, the Governor invited Ted Service and me to breakfast at Government House. We discussed Mrs. Tawes' cookbook, but since people mostly did not know of Ted's connection with it at that time, rumors ran wild.

Lest you fear that this venture into the wild, wild world of political party-going went unnoticed back home or at my place of work, I received two reactions.

A lady from the Democratic Advocate, who had been kind to me in her column prior to my election as a Republican delegate, became downright ungenerous in her next column. In her column called 'Bit by Bit by Slim' she raised the question of where the money had come from to pay for the party, and why I had thrown such a party in Annapolis.

I never bothered to reply to the attack, but history says I received no money from anybody. It wasn't even left over donated money from my campaign. I'd raised no funds and had paid for all of my election expenses out of my own pocket.

My Supervisor at Singer felt that I should have the party, so he effectively advanced me the money to pay for it, then deducted the sum from my bonus. In short, I received my normal bonus minus a thousand dollars.

Any Legislator's career is a history of battles won and battles lost. In 1969, I may have lost more than I won. I can't really be sure. Among the bills I introduced was one designed to provide help to any impaired witness who had to testify in court. Specifically, it called for the provision of interpreters suffering deafness or an other handicap making it difficult for him to understand the English language or to communicate.

Another bill was designed to exempt certain non-profit organizations from paying real estate taxes. In yet another case, I opposed a bill designed to increase taxes on beer sold in Carroll County. I was joined in this effort by 47 Carroll Countians who journeyed to Annapolis to protest the bill.

A bill I introduced twice was designed to outlaw conflict of interest on the part of officials or employees of the County who engaged in a business for profit selling to or contracting with the County Government. My chief opponent was Scott Bair. His Brother-in-law was my colleague in the Legislature, Richard Matthews. Matthew's refusal to support the bill killed it

.

One newspaper editorial summarized the 1969 impact as follows:

"There were a fairly large number of constructive bills introduced by the county delegates land, in comparison with the previous year, the county delegation's output was exceptional.

"Special praise goes to Delegate Jacob M. Yingling, who as usual submitted the most bills, and, in this writer's judgment, the best bills. It was Yingling , as one school observer mentioned this week, who insured that Carroll County gets kindergarten next year (a move was on to have a phase in program for counties now without kindergartens, of which there are 7 in the State). Jake stopped it."

I feel that in 1970 I made a major contribution to the County by introducing a bill that called for the creation of a Director of Finance position for Carroll County. The Director of Finance would have the overall supervision and responsibility for administering county finances as well as advising the County Commissioners on all fiscal questions. The bill passed.

What many people don't understand is the way in which out of session discussions influence the course of legislation. This was especially true in the case of my perception of a drug abuse situation existing in the County as well as in the need for legislation enabling the issuance of school construction bonds. Both issues were debated in open meetings with strong opposition coming from then Senator Smelser. He objected strongly to taking action in advance of the actual need. Here, as in many other cases, my view of the future, in retrospect, was much clearer than that of my opponents. Many of them were advocates of the type of legislative action based on a philosophy of "if it ain't broke don't fix it" or "if we give them the money too soon they'll just spend it. **In retrospect, I now realize that during my legislative days, I was often ahead of my time on social and cultural issues.**

On August 29,1972 I made a crucial decision. I decided to leave the legislature for what I felt to be a better opportunity as is explained in the following letter.

Honorable Thomas Hunter Lowe, Speaker
Maryland House of Delegates
Annapolis, Maryland 21404

Dear Tom:

I will be vacating my seat in the House of Delegates for Carroll County, as of September 11, 1972. I have accepted the position of Assistant Secretary for the Department of Economic and Community Development.

My association with the Maryland General Assembly has been a very rewarding and challenging one. In my new position I'm looking forward to continuing relationships.

Sincerely,

Jacob M. Yingling

Copy to: Frank Arnold, Chairman, Republican State Central Committee of Carroll County

My new duties would permit me to move into the State Government at a level where I would be exposed to the actual governance of the State. It would give me hands on experience in the management of a number of on-going operations. Initially, I would be responsible for Personnel and Budgets. Then I was placed in charge of the Division of Community Development. This was concerned with a variety of Departments such as: Codes Administration, Commission on Afro-American and Indian History and Culture, Development Financing Program, Local Development Assistance, Maryland Arts Council, Maryland Bicentennial Commission, Maryland Historical Trust, Maryland Home Financing Program, and the St. Mary's City Commission. My final assignment in government was as Assistant Secretary, Economic Development. In this job I was responsible for: Business and Industrial Development, The Maryland Industrial Development Financing Authority, Office of Minority Business Enterprise, Seafood Marketing Authority, and Tourist Development

In all three of these roles, I found my experience with banks, my education as a history major, and my employment in industry to be invaluable. In addition to my declared duties, I, also, was fortunate to receive other assignments which exposed me to an even wider variety of operations within our multi-faceted State government.

I have focused on the actual functioning of the Legislature and avoided spending time on the climate within which many of our discussions took place. The Civil Rights Movement and the Vietnam War were constantly present in our minds if not officially noted.

During the early Sixties, the country came close to experiencing a 'black revolt'. SNCC, CORE, Martin Luther King and the Civil Rights Movement created daily headlines. Maryland was not Mississippi but neither was it immune to the pressures generated by the various protest actions.

In the late Sixties the country was fixated on the pros and cons of fighting the Vietnam War. In the fall of 1967, the war protests came home to Baltimore. Father Phillip Berrigan and friends invaded a draft office in Baltimore and drenched the draft records in blood. The following May, joined by his brother, Daniel, Father Berrigan did it again. This time they were joined by seven other people who helped them invade a draft office in Catonsville, Maryland, remove and publicly burn draft records. These particular protestors became known as 'The Catonsville Nine'.

Although the Catholic priests and nuns were somewhat unexpected protestors, the real action generally focused on college students and their militancy. These student protests climaxed in the spring of 1970 when President Nixon ordered the invasion of Cambodia. This gave rise to the unfortunate shots fired at students by National Guardsmen called to put down a student protest at Kent State University in Ohio. Following the shootings at Kent State, four hundred other campuses were struck by their students.

The saga of the Berrigans and some of their co-protestors such as a former Nun, Mary Moylan, are the stuff of heroic fiction. If I had had the creative inspiration to try that mode of expression then, I might have written an inspired movie script and become famous.

Instead, I was still intrigued by the political maneuvering which surrounded me. For example, in 1965, I sat in on the edges of serious discussions which led some people to national office. I've often thought that – had I known then, what I know now – as the gurus would have it, I too might have progressed through the looking glass into the never -never land of national politics to which every young politician aspires.

"What if?" is a game played in today's world by many people. There is even a recent book which explores the changes that would have occurred on various battlefields if different decisions and circumstances had prevailed. The same game is often played when we talk about world and national leaders. For example, what would have happened if FDR had died of his polio? If Martin Luther had died before he posted his edicts on that Church in Nantes would there have been a Martin Luther King? What if Churchill had turned down his selection to be Prime Minister because he opposed the War? What if Hitler had not miscalculated and attacked Russia? Well, then, let me pose a 'What If' from my own political past.

The people are real. The incidents actually happened. The What If comes in when you ask what would have happened had a chain of decisions been made differently. My What If starts with my being asked to speak at a meeting held on September 25, 1965. The meeting was the 1965 Annual Maryland Republican Policy Conference.

MY OWN PERSONAL 'WHAT IF'

The meeting began at 9 AM in the Wedgewood Room of the Emerson Hotel. on Saturday, September 25, 1965. This meeting had been preceded by a previous meeting held on September 10, 1965 in the Caswell Room of the Lord Baltimore Hotel. Both were public meetings and I was a scheduled speaker at each.

The purpose of the first meeting was to take testimony concerning half a dozen bread and butter political issues facing Maryland voters. The purpose was to hear testimony and then distill the various statements down into a statement of Republican party attitudes. The lead off speaker for the first meeting was Rogers C.B. Morton of Maryland's First District. At this meeting the chairman announced the names of the six subcommittee chairmen who would direct the policy positions in: natural resources; health; economic development; taxes and finance; transportation; and education.

The purpose of the second meeting was to develop a strategy for the 1966 election and preview the potential candidates for Governor. The lead-off speaker for this meeting was Spiro Agnew, who was then the Baltimore County Executive. I spoke as a witness at this meeting.

Several names were mentioned as possible candidates for Governor. These included: J. Glenn Beall, Minority Leader and Delegate from Allegheny County. He was a possible all right but he wanted to run for Congress. A loss in the race for Governor might unfavorably impact those chances. A second possibility was Stanley Blair of Harford County but, as the discussion proceeded, it turned out that the party wanted him to run against Senator James, the President of the Maryland Senate, in the next election. Blair was later named as a Federal Judge by Nixon.

Several others, for good if differing reasons did not care to run. Some did not want to surrender safe seats. Others did not want to be cannon fodder and suffer a probable loss to the superior Democratic registration numbers.

I indicated I would be interested since I had been speaking at fund-raisers throughout the state and had been received favorably. I had received some state-wide interest and had been given promises of financial support.

Spiro Agnew was also very interested since he had no chance of being re-elected to a second term as Baltimore County Executive. He, however, had been receiving financial support from Greeks in and out of the state.

I was told I could easily be re-elected in Carroll County and should not sacrifice myself at this early stage of my career. I, of course did not see running for Governor as a sacrifice. Win or lose, I would have advanced considerably just by running.

With no other opposition, Agnew thus became the candidate for Governor on the Republican ticket.

On the Democratic side a primary fight developed among Tom Finian, the Attorney General, Carlton Sickles, a Congressman from Prince George County and George Mahoney, a Baltimore County resident. It was thought Finian would win but he and Sickles canceled each other out and George Mahoney won the Democratic Primary. In the General Election, Mahoney campaigned with a motto "Your Home is Your Castle". This angered the blacks in Baltimore City and they voted for Agnew

Had I been the candidate, I would have been elected Governor. I had strong support in the black community especially with black educators.

The next series of events went as follows. Rogers Morton became Chairman of the Republican National Committee. Nixon asked him to become his running mate. Rogers declined, but was given the privilege of picking Nixon's running mate. He chose the Governor of Maryland. Had I been the Governor, I would have ended up VP of the United States.

As history records, Agnew was forced to resign when he pleaded guilty to income tax invasion. He had not paid taxes on some alleged kickbacks.

That would not have been the case for me and I would have remained VP. When Nixon resigned, I would have become the President of the United States, not Gerald Ford.

I realize it may take a lot of imagination for anyone to conceive of this actually happening, but it would not have been the strangest event in our political history. At the very least this is a story for my Grandchildren relating to them how Grandpop might have become President of the United States.

**Governor of North Carolina (James E. Holshouser),
Gordon Halleck, and Jake at Seafood Conclave
in North Carolina.**

OTHER ANNAPOLIS YEARS

Other roles which I fulfilled during my time in State Government included:

Committee on the Preservation of Agricultural Land, 1973-74

Director and official representative of Maryland for Trade Missions, 1976

Committee Member, Maryland Building Code for the Handicapped and aged, 1977-79

Chairman, Special study committee Life Care Contracts, 1978

Director of Sheltered Housing, State Office on Aging, 1977-79

Waste to Energy Study Commission, 1993-94

In many ways my most fascinating assignment, Director of Trade Missions, came about almost by default. Generally, Trade Missions are headed by the Governor and the delegation includes invited important businessmen from the State. The purpose of the mission, of course, is to secure and attract overseas business for the State.

I was appointed because Governor Mandel was involved in legal problems. These made his leaving the country very difficult. Why they bypassed my boss, I'm not sure, but he may also have had personal problems at that time. Or it may have been as simple as funding. The monies necessary to mount a Trade Mission are approved at a very high level. At that time it was well known that I was looked on favorably by both the Governor and the Board of Public Works.

The planned first trip was to the Middle East. I, and some other members of the Delegation, attended briefings at the State Department and the Department of Commerce in Washington. In these, we were instructed in the customs and political correctness practices to be observed while in the various host countries. On that first overseas trip we visited Iran, Kuwait, Syria and Saudi Arabia.

In Iran, I made friends with a number of officials who later lost their lives to the takeover of the Embassy. At that time we were received graciously and I have many fond memories of Iran.

While in Tehran, the capital, I visited the school for the deaf. This was dear to my heart since I was, at that time, a member of the board of the Board for Visitors for the Maryland School for the Deaf. The head of the department responsible for teaching deaf education at Western Maryland College had told me about a lady in Tehran who was married to an international banker. She was reported to be active in the Iranian School for the Deaf. I suggested that it might be useful for me to drop by and visit with her.

When I called, I found that the husband was out of the country on business, but the Lady took me to their country club for lunch.

Afterwards, we visited the School for the Deaf. At her suggestion, I visited mainly with the five and six year olds. They spoke only Farsi and I spoke only English, but he had no difficulty communicating. They could sign, and although my signing back was limited, they seemed to understand. These very bright-eyed Iranian children stood in line to come up and shake my hand and say 'hello'.

I had remembered to bring some miniature Hershey chocolate bars and packs of chewing gum with me. I was able to give each child some chocolate and a single stick of gum. Those huge, expressive eyes lit up and their faces glowed. It was, for me, a totally endearing moment.

I've often looked back and wondered, in view of our stormy relationships with Iran, where those wonderful children have gone and what they might have accomplished. I've even dared to hope that one moment of meeting an American who was obviously not 'the Great Satan' might have helped shaped a friendlier attitude toward us.

In Iran, I encountered a practice which seems to be quite common in certain parts of Europe. A friend has spoken of a similar event in Barcelona.

On arrival at the hotel, I was escorted to a suite of rooms.. For whatever reason, perhaps because I was head of the Delegation, I was often given the suite at the cost of one room. In this case, on entering the second room of the suite, I encountered a beautiful young lady. I found she spoke perfect English when I told her that I would leave while she vacated the suite. I had misunderstood. I had believed she had been delayed in checking out.

"I can't do that, Mister Sir. I go with the suite."

"Well, Ma'am. I appreciate the offer, but I can't accept it."

"I can't leave. I just can't. If you force me out, they will think I have done something wrong. They will be displeased with me." She began crying loudly.\

"I'll take care of it." I said and picked up the phone. When the Manager arrived at the room, I explained my dilemma.

"I'm a happily married man and this would not be an acceptable arrangement back home. I have to decline the offer with thanks for your thoughtfulness, but I must decline. Please do not penalize the Lady. She behaved most correctly."

My friend's case was even a touch more complicated since he had his wife traveling with him. They were told the room was not yet made up. They had to sit in the lobby and wait while the reluctant-to-leave Catalan was beseeched to stop screaming and dragged from the suite. My friend didn't fully learn what had happened until he visited his client in Barcelona at their offices the next day. This was apparently normal business practice for the Spanish firm with which he was dealing.

The Shah was still in power in Iran at the time of my visit. We were entertained at very high levels by his staff, although he, himself, was not available.

Our reception in Kuwait was both warm and fascinating. We did have an opportunity to meet with the Emir. This occurred in a large room occupied by a number of what I presumed to be security guards dressed in Arabic robes. They were sitting about with their legs crossed and their rifles nearby. They continued to sit in place looking stoic and uninterested during our entire conversation with the Emir and his ministers.

We were served very strong coffee. I, unfortunately, drank mine very fast so that I would get rid of it. Bad move! As fast as I emptied the demitasse cup in which it was served, it was refilled. I had been warned that it would be impolite not to consume whatever we were served. I later learned that when you don't want any more, you put the cup down and jiggle it a bit.

Before I left the States, I had been given a medallion to present to the Emir. One side represented the United States Seal and the other had to do with peace and commerce. I'd guessed its value to be around twenty-five dollars. At an appropriate moment during the conversation, I presented this to the Emir. He seemed most appreciative.

Back at my hotel, I received a call from a representative of the Emir. He told me how much the Emir had appreciated the gift and asked if he could come by and present me with a similar token of his regard. As a precaution, I called John Gatch, our advance man, to be sure it was alright for me to accept the gift. John was the former charge d'affaires in Bahrein. He knew the middle east customs well. He advised me to receive the delegation.

When he saw what the delegation gave me, his only comment was 'Holy Hell'! They had given me a gold medallion about three inches in diameter and a half inch thick. Since I was not under any restrictions from the State Department, I kept the gift and still have it today. I made other visits to Kuwait, but that first one is the one which lingers most in my memory.

As a follow up I should mention an accidental encounter which occurred several years later.

In the late 1980's I attended an international medical conference in Williamsburg, Virginia as a representative of St. Joseph's Hospital. When the conference adjourned, I, among many other conference attendees, assembled to share a conference sponsored bus ride to the airport. When the bus was almost ready to depart, I notice a lady carrying two heavy bags running toward it. The bus driver stopped and waited but made no move to get off and help the lady with her luggage. I jumped down and helped her board the bus. I then stowed her luggage for her and found her a seat across the aisle from me. Since it seemed appropriate, I spoke back to her when she thanked me.

"Did you enjoy the conference?" I asked. I had seen by her tag that she was a doctor. Her clothing was definitely Middle Eastern or East Indian. "I assume you're not from the States."

"That is right. I'm from a country you probably never heard of – Kuwait."

"Not really true." I replied with a smile. "I've visited Kuwait several times. I met some wonderful people there."

"Oh, that's a surprise. Who did you meet? Officials?"

"Yes. Several ministers. Relating that to this conference, one of them was the Minister of Health."

"A coincidence, Sir. That is my husband. He, too, is a doctor." With that, she fished in her purse and pulled out a card. It was her husband's card. "If you visit Kuwait again, please show that card to my husband. He will know of the courtesy you have extended to me."

I thought later how living in a sequestered society like that of Kuwait would have been inhibiting to anyone raised in America. There is no way I could have even spoken to this woman in her own country. She would have been veiled and sequestered. I knew that she understood that well also, but had enjoyed the opportunity to talk freely with me on that bus.

In retrospect, it seems ironic that our most peaceful and rewarding visit was to Kuwait which later became Iraq's target in the Gulf War. Conversely, our visits to Lebanon and Syria turned out to be anything but peaceful.

We flew into Beirut on a Japanese Airlines commercial flight. As it turned out, the only people aboard were Japanese officials who'd been sent to help evacuate their embassy because of the Palestinian induced fighting. In fact, when we landed, there was fighting taking place at the edge of the airport. When they raised the ramp and opened the door, I found myself confronted by a scruffy looking man with a rifle. He stuck the rifle barrel in my gut and demanded to know who I was and why I was there.

"We're an official Unites States Delegation passing through on a trade mission." That got argued back and forth while the Japanese disembarked. Finally, we were permitted to resume our seats and the plane took off.

On another trip, while we were in Kuwait and planning to move on to Syria, we received an advisory through the Embassy. It said we might want to cancel the trip because the Syrians were considered to be aiding the Palestinians. After calls back to the States and consultation with the State Department, they indicated that it might be alright to proceed, but it was our own decision. I decided to push on to Damascus. As it turned out, it was a really good decision.

When the delegation arrived in Damascus, we were greeted warmly by Ambassador Richard Murphy and his wife. Later, Ambassador Murphy became Assistant Secretary for the Middle East in the State Department and top advisor to the Administration during the Gulf War.

Although we had been assured that our visit was safe, there was an armed guard posted beside the room in which I stayed. I presume, since there were no other guards in evidence, this was because I was nominally the head of the delegation. I don't know whether the guard was watching me or protecting me, but he followed me everywhere I went. In truth, he remained at a distinct distance, never interfered and certainly never spoke to me. Nor did I to him.

I was asked to address the local Chamber of Commerce. This wan not like any Chamber of Commerce I'd ever encountered in the United States. The room contained the top Syrian leadership, the movers and shakers of the country. There were even some Generals as well as people identified to me as Government Ministers. I started out what I thought was a diplomatic approach to the need for international commerce and the role commerce played in international peace.

Suddenly, one man jumped to his feet and shouted at me.

"Secretary Yingling! Why are you really here? What is your secret mission?"

"Sir!" I protested. "As I just said, I am here to promote commerce and trade between our countries."

"You're from Maryland, aren't you?"

"Yes I am."

"You have a Jewish Governor!"

"We do indeed. Governor Mandel certainly is Jewish."

"Well, why would a Jewish Governor want to do business with an Arab country?

"Listen to me. Please! The best way I can explain is that he is Governor of all our people. We have a lot of Arabs living in Maryland. We have many different nationalities living in Maryland and in the Unites States. We try not to distinguish between religious beliefs or races. Furthermore, even though Governor Mandel is Jewish, he is not a Zionist. In addition to that, we do have an Arab in the Maryland cabinet."

I noticed that the man had been taken aback by my defense. He'd fallen silent so I continued

"Please, my friend. Listen to me. That Arab is a personal friend of mine. He is a personal friend of the Governor's. He has the complete confidence of the Governor or he would not be the Secretary of Planning for the State of Maryland. My friend's name is Vladimir Wahbe."

At the point, when I pronounced 'Vladimir Wahbe', a large chant broke out from the back of the room. People jumped to their feet. They thrust their hands into the air and shouted: "Wahbe, Wahbe, Wahbe."

I almost panicked. Where's my guard now, I wondered. Why are those people streaming down the aisles? They're coming for me, right for me. What stupid convention did I violate now? I thought the State Department briefing had covered everything I could possibly do wrong.

Then, I noticed that everyone in the room, except me, was smiling and that the confusion was backing down. I winced as yet another man jumped to his feet and began waving the crowd to silence. Then, he spoke directly to me in perfect English.

"Secretary Yingling, you probably are slightly shocked at our demonstration, but please understand. Vladimir Wahbe is a name we respect in this country. He was Minister of Planning for Damascus, then for the entire country of Syria. He is greatly respected and still loved. He had family in this very area."

Another man, one who looked exactly like Sidney Greenstreet on a good day, then stood and asked:

"May I please come up to the podium?" He didn't wait for an answer but came up immediately. He put his arms around me and kissed me on both cheeks.

"You are very welcome. Anything we can do for you in Damascus will be done. Just please let us know."

On my returns to the States, I received a call from Val Wahbe.

"Jake, " he asked. "What did you do to those people in Damascus?" He laughed, then continued. "They called me from Syria just to tell me how pleased they were with your speech."

On other trips to Kuwait the delegations began to see their business people in attendance. That however did not really change in Syria. They did, however, readily respond to the one request I mentioned. I told them I was especially interested in exploring the road the Prophet Paul had taken to Damascus.

I was escorted to the road where history indicates Paul was knocked off his donkey, At this point I could sense that I was actually treading in Paul's footsteps. Then, they took me to the prison where he had been incarcerated and showed me how, after 2000 years, you could still see the difference in the bricks where friends of his had made a hole in the wall and helped him escape.

"See," pointed out the Guide." Look how different the bricks are where the hole was punched in the wall. Had he not escaped, he would have been executed."

I do not consider myself to be deeply religious, but this sense of history certainly brought more reality to the Bible than I'd ever felt before. In a personal sense, following Paul's footsteps was a tremendously religious experience. "In Syria" I was told. "There is still an active Christian community which offers the mass in Arabic."

Never in any of the Arab countries we visited did I really experience any sense of being considered an Ugly American. Even the places most likely to be wary of ugly Americans received us warmly and had good things to say about the United States.

SHELTERED HOUSING

In spring of 1977, I received a call from the Office on Aging. I was told the Legislature had enacted legislation to provide Sheltered Housing in Maryland. They needed someone to implement the legislation and set up the rules and regulations to control it. I was told that Acting Governor Blair Lee had approved my heading the effort.

I provided a manual of operations and set up the ground rules. After this was done I approved funding several operations throughout Maryland. The program immediately began to attract national attention. As a result I was invited to give seminars and attend workshops all over the U. S. I spoke to the National Conference of Mayors as well a other national and state organizations. I even had an invitation for Hawaii to tell them about our system. I was directly instrumental in helping the Ohio legislature pass similar legislation by testifying at their committee hearing.

All in all, this provided me with a superb opportunity to expand my personal horizons with hands-on work. I spoke at conferences in a number of States, including New Jersey, Vermont. New Hampshire, Connecticut, and Ohio. I also fulfilled a number of major speaking engagements before groups such as the National Conference of Mayors and the Ohio Legislature. We received a large number of both inquiries and visitors. The furthest visitor came from Hawaii and stayed with us for nearly two weeks. The bulk of our visitors, of course, came from right here in Maryland and involved a wide variety of people, everyone from officials from municipalities and architects concerned about building standards.

In Ohio the bill was strongly supported by the International Brotherhood of Teamsters. They felt the bill ultimately passed by the Ohio Legislature was critical to the long term care of their membership. They pulled out all the stops to make it happen. The effort was supervised by Jackie Presser, International Vice President and involved Mister Joseph Knight from their Democratic Republican Voter Education unit which is the political voice of the Teamsters, as well as Paul Locigno, who was the Director of Research for the Ohio Conference of Teamsters. The Bill was strongly supported by the Speaker Pro Tem of the House.

As passed their bill was strongly based on our work in Maryland.

Jacob M. Yingling
Assistant Secretary for Economic Development
Maryland Department of Economic and
Community Development
1748 Forest Drive, Annapolis, Maryland 21401

Jacob M. Yingling is the official Maryland representative for the Trade Mission. As an Assistant Secretary of the Maryland Department of Economic and Community Development since 1972, he is involved on a daily basis with promoting Maryland as an ideal location for business and industry. He is a graduate of Gettysburg College and a former Maryland Legislator. He has had wide management experience in private industry as well as State Government.

Mr. Yingling will serve as spokesman for the Maryland Trade Mission. He will be able to answer questions about the State of Maryland and the capabilities of Maryland firms and institutions active in health care delivery systems.

هو الممثل الرسمي لولاية ماريلاند في البعثة التجارية ۰ وبما أنه مساعد لوزير التنمية الإقتصادية والإجتماعية منذ عام ۱۹۷۲ فان من صلب مسؤوليته أن يعمل على جعل ماريلاند مكانا مثاليا للصناعة والإعمال ۰

والسيد ينتفع بخريج كلية غيتسبورغ (ولاية بنسلفانيا) وعضو سابق في مجلس النواب في ماريلاند ، وهو يتمتع بخبرة إدارية واسعة في القطاع الصناعي كما في القطاع العام ۰ وبصفته الناطق بلسان بعثة ماريلاند التجارية فهو سيجيب عن كل سؤال يتعلق بالولاية وبامكانيات الشركات والمؤسسات العاملة فيها من حيث توريد أجهزة العناية الصحية ۰

جكوب، ينگلنگ ابینگ نما ایند و رسمی میسیون بازرگا نی مریلنداست ۰ ا ،مان ن بعنوان ن معاون ن ادار و توسعه ا قصادی واجتماعی مسیر یلند فرضا البسته ویروزا ند خودا رسال ۱۹۷۲ مریلنگرابه ینهمنستطفیه ا یده اآل بازرگا نی ومنعی نرفی داده ا ند ۱۰ ،مان ن فارع ا لتحصیل ازکالج گیتسبرگمنتدیدیا یقا صومیتتسهفنند مریلندبوده ا ند ۰ ا ،مان نهم درماویتماتح بح صوبی ومن فرانی تجربسسه ا ی وسیع دارند ۰

آا ویینگله ابینگ بعثرا ن متحنگری میسیون بازرگا نی مسیر یلند کارخواهندکرد ۰ ا ،مان ن میتوا نتدبه اوگرگوته پرسخیدرمورد ا یساله ت مریلندوتوان نا نی کمپا نی ها ی مریلندوموسسا تنعان نفرا خبسسسام سیستم ها ی بهداشتنی یاسخ دهند ۰

Dr. Abdul Rahman A. Al - Awadi
Minister of Public Health

P. O. Box 5
Tel. 433285

Kuwait

Brochure in Farsi and Arabic prepared for trade mission to the Middle East.
See Page 147-8 for calling card information.

A. Iranian bodyguards.
B. Outside U.S. Embassy in Saudi Arabia.
C. Outside King Faisal Hospital in Saudi Arabia.

OTHER POLITICAL PEOPLE AND PLACES

During my time in the Legislature and in State Government, I met everyone from cleaning people to Governors from many States, Legislators from other States, Vice Presidents, Presidents, Ambassadors and foreign dignitaries, and many many members from both houses of Congress. Almost without exception, I was received courteously and as promptly as circumstances permitted. In a sense this began before I really had accomplished much of anything in my own right.

As an example, the Carroll County Republican Club wanted a speaker for an important event. At that time I was President of the Club. Alvie Spencer and I procured an appointment with Everett Dirkson in his office in Washiington. At that time, Senator Dirkson was minority leader in the Senate. The receptionist told us there'd be about a twenty minute delay since he was momentarily busy. Almost on the twenty minute mark, the inner door burst open and there was Everett Dirkson in person.

His hair, his mannerisms, his very carriage immediately told you that this was a man of special significance. He came right over to us, introduced himself warmly, and apologized for the delay.

"Mr. Yingling, you don't know how much I appreciate you waiting for me." He then looked aver at his Secretary. "Mary," he said, "Unless the President calls, this time is Mr. Yingling's. I don't wish to be disturbed." I felt sure this was a standard method for impressing visitors, but, none the less, I found it well done.

In the course of my legislative work, I met Presidents Nixon, Johnson and Ford, all before they became President. All carried themselves differently, and they looked nothing alike, but all possessed that same aura of significance which seemed to hover about Senator Dirkson. I've labeled it in my own mind as the 'glow of importance'. All of these men had the ability to transmit this glow to the people with whom they were speaking. They never looked beyond you. They looked right at you. At that moment, you, too, felt important.

A close friend of mine who had reason to visit the White House on rare occasions understood this transfer of the aura effect. He said it showed for him in the way he was treated after spending considerable time with President Johnson in his office.

"Everybody I passed in the hall as I was leaving the West Wing smiled. They didn't know who I was or why I was there, but they knew I had just spent over an hour tete a tete with the President. That cloaked me with a totally unjustified sense of importance."

During the summer of 1964, prior to the presidential election, I attended a book exhibit in Washington. This was an annual event. The evening before the exhibit, the bookmen from the various companies had dinner together. Everybody worked the floor the next day. On the floor, they had a good chance to meet with the attending teachers and school administrators. As was my custom, I took time off to go over to the hill and talk with some of the members of Congress that I knew. As a matter of political courtesy, I always spent time with their staff members. Naturally, I had more Republican than Democratic contacts.

This day I made an early visit to a staff member in Kansas Senator Carlson's office. At that time Bob Dole was the junior senator and Carlson the senior.

"I'm in town for a book exhibit tomorrow." I explained.

"Oh, you're staying over tonight, then?" Do you have any plans for the evening?"

"I'll just be going to dinner with the salesmen for other companies tonight." Although I'd never deceived anyone about what level job I held, the staff man also knew I was a Republican member of the Maryland Legislature.

"How would you like to try something just a bit more exciting? I can get you a ticket to the Cherry Blossom Festival Ball."

"Oh, that sounds really nice." I replied. "But I don't have my tux here. I just don't think I could get it down here in time for tonight."

"Jake, that's not a problem. Give me your sizes. We'll get you a tux and deliver it to your hotel along with a ticket to the ball."

Well, this was just too good an opportunity to turn down. I knew this would give me an opportunity to socialize at a very high level of Washington society. I was right. When I arrived at the ball, I found my seating was with the family of Senator Goldwater.

The Cherry Blossom Festival then was a little different than it is today. They had a large wheel with about fifty young ladies' names on it. The wheel was spun and wherever it stopped, that person became the Queen. Well, all that folderol aside, the food was good and the company great. It definitely was the most exposure I ever had to the power elite of Washington at one time.

Senator Carlson's staffer took me to other tables and introduced me as 'The Honorable Jacob Yingling from Maryland'. I was warmly greeted and enjoyed myself immensely. I really floated back to my hotel on a cloud of cherry blossoms.

The next morning, before I took the tux back to the rental agency, I went downstairs to have breakfast with some of my competitors.

"Where were you for dinner, Jake?"

"Oh, I didn't feel well and just went to bed early."

"We know better than that, Jake. You're lying in your teeth."

I didn't think they could possibly know I'd been to the Cherry Blossom Festival ball and I repeated my story.

"Knock it off, Jake. We saw you on TV."

I hadn't realized the event was televised. That concerned me because I knew my wife would have wanted to go if she'd known about it. I called Genny and asked her what she'd done that night.

"I watched the Cherry Blossom Festival Ball on TV, but I got sleepy and turned it off early." I don't know that she and I have ever discussed this, but, by now, it should be all resolved. At the time I had a really guilty conscience. My excuse to myself was that I'd been given just the one ticket.

I was fortunate to meet a number of highly regarded Congressmen and get to spend enough time with them to have a sense of them as people. These included Senator Montoya of New Mexico and his colleague, Senator Anderson. I met Senator Anderson at a time when his career was winding down. I greatly enjoyed his stories about having been one of Harry Truman's poker playing cronies.

One person I came to know very well was Adam Clayton Powell. I met with him when he was Chairman of the Education and Labor Committee. He was the only black chairman at that time. Although he was extraordinarily capable, he was also arrogant and flamboyant. These traits agitated many of his colleagues. Eventually, he was censured and dismissed from Congress. His constituents, however, reelected him and he resumed his seat. He never regained the power he'd once had. My best memory of him is how he loved to go fishing in Bimini. He had a home there and loved to go bone fishing. He suggested I might visit him and join in the fishing but I never did and I regret that. It would have been a blast.

I had many encounters with Nixon. I attended several fund raising dinners for him after he was VP, and after his defeat as Governor of California, but before his 1968 candidacy for President. I had a number of opportunities go engage in small talk, but we never discussed anything of earth shaking importance.

One on one, Nixon was a very engaging man, but he always seemed to be in a hurry. Whenever I walked up to him to shake his hand and say 'hello', he always seemed to be looking over my shoulder or glancing at someone else.. I never felt I had his undivided attention. Most politicians develop the ability to make you feel that at that one moment when you greet them, you are the most important person in their lives. Nixon did not.

He was obviously intelligent, well versed in almost any topic that arose, and could emit charm, but only when he chose. In retrospect, I have to believe that Nixon was his own worst enemy. I sometimes thought he tried to appear tougher than he really was. He actually swore as much as Johnson, but Johnson almost engulfed you when he first met you. You could say 'no' to Dick Nixon without it troubling you. You could not do this to Lyndon Johnson.

Of course, the whole Texas crowd was different. I always felt they figured they had to hang together or get hung separately. To me, it was a never a case of Democrats versus Republicans as much as Texas versus the rest of the nation. I met Jim Wright from Dallas-Fort Worth early on because my boss, Dick Bobbitt, was from Texas. His mother had been very active in Wright's campaign. Dick always made checking his traps with the Texas Delegation well worth the effort. In those days the Texas Delegation had the reputation of being a real powerhouse in Washington. Dick wanted to be sure I understood how best to approach them.

To tell the truth, I felt much more affinity for Nelson Rockefeller than for the Texas people. For me, Rockefeller had far more to offer than Barry Goldwater. Rockefeller had good experience. He was a former Governor of New York, was experienced in the world scene, and came from a distinguished family. I felt he was much better equipped to be President than Goldwater.

I supported Rockefeller. On several occasions he sent his private plane to Annapolis to carry several of us to New York for special get-togethers. That plane carried the elite of the Republican party in Maryland to New York. On one trip the turbulence got through to me. It was a stormy day and the plane was a small two prop job which seemed determined to find the worst of the weather. By the time we reached New York, I was totally airsick and couldn't even walk.

This was pointed out to the Governor. He immediately assigned a nurse to care for me. I was taken aside and dosed up with medications to combat the air sickness. Later, I was able to return to the meeting.

When I entered the room, Rockefeller stopped what he was doing, came over and asked if there was anything further he could do for me. This, I felt, was a very special gesture from a very great man.

Unfortunately, as time passed, the party nominated Mister Goldwater and Nelson Rockefeller turned to other matters. He later became VP on the ticket with Mr. Ford. During the interim, I was fortunate to be invited to meet with he and his wife, Happy, in the home they maintained in northwest Washington.

I first met President Ford when he was the representative to Congress from Grand Rapids, Michigan. I was on the board of an insurance company headquartered there and met him in that role at an insurance company special event.

As it turned out, I felt that Ford did a good job for the country. He healed the divisiveness which had arisen over Nixon's actions. It would have been interesting to see what kind of a legacy he would have left with another four years under his belt. I really thought he was going to beat Carter. I was traveling in the Middle East at the time and everybody I met, in foreign embassies as well as our diplomats abroad, predicted Ford's probable victory. I never found him being condemned for pardoning Nixon the way some politicians in the States did. I'm not sure that act was the ultimate reason for Ford's defeat but I feel innate hatred for Nixon did contribute to it.

Of course, Ford, even though President, was not really well known. And it must have been difficult to run an aggressive, forward looking campaign while he was still busy fighting off attacks on his Nixon dominated past from the rear.

A PERSONAL NOTE

THROUGHOUT MY CAREER, WHETHER ACTING AS A BUSINESSMAN, AN INVESTOR, A POLITICIAN OR AN EMPLOYEE OF THE STATE, I HAVE BEEN ATTACKED BY NAYSAYERS OF ONE SORT OR ANOTHER.

Mostly, my "enemies", their word not mine, (I preferred 'opponent or opposition') took out after me because I was on the side of an issue that differed from theirs. Not infrequently, my attitude was taken in protest at what I considered to be an illegal or unfortunate effort to gain profit at the expense of me or some innocent third party.

While I consider myself to be fiscally conservative both as a manager and an investor, I do speak out freely in the political arena or when I encounter financial duplicity. I know I can be stubborn when I am convinced that my stand is on the side of the angels. People I considered to be siding with the Devil deplored my holy approach and frequently said so. I am proud to say I won the majority of such conflicts.

People who were in such conflicts with me have long wondered precisely what I thought of their tactics. Always before I was reluctant to be totally truthful with them for I feared they'd not understand or appreciate the

truth. Now, since they know of whom I speak, I direct their attention to page 190. This will spell out what I truly thought of them and how I think of them now.

WHAT DOES IT ALL ADD UP TO?

In conclusion, the first thing that comes to mind is that when it's all said and done, I call myself a 'spiritual person', that is not to say 'religious', nor 'born again', nor 'born in the blood of the lamb'.

Even though I have always felt it was somewhat significant that my first American ancestor was named Christian, I have never believed I was born to be locked into a particular church as much as into a faith in God. I've always seen Jesus as a rebel against the Jewish hierarchy of his day, not necessarily as someone who intentionally founded a 'different' religion. If anyone actually founded Christianity, in my opinion it was Paul.

What I feel this adds up to is that I believe in a Universal God whose works I have observed throughout my entire life. I believe that every man is truly my brother and that the Universal God created all of us. I believe I have an obligation to recognize the rights of my brothers while hoping that they, in return, will recognize mine. Beyond this, while I recognize scientific truths such as the bulk of evolutionary theory and the part genetic dispositions play in our lives, I must go further and say that the order I perceive in the universe cannot have occurred by accident. Where there is order, I tend to see the hand of God.

All of my life I have questioned the authoritative speakers who proclaim rigidity of belief and manifest knowledge they cannot reasonably possess. This was indeed the circumstance which resulted in the wrongful persecution of Galileo by the Catholic Church. These 'declared' authoritarianists' cannot tolerate non-agreement nor dissident points which call their beliefs into question. I learned as a child that the people in control want agreement, not questions.

I attended Catholic School and served as an altar boy in the Parish Church. Both of these situations led to questions. These questions angered both the Nuns who taught in the school and the Priests who officiated at Mass.

I'm not sure what genetic formula led to my constant pursuit of the truth, but it evidenced itself early. Perhaps it was partly my Father's determination to survive the Depression and see me into college. Perhaps it was my Mother's aggressive pursuit of ways to accomplish this. More gently, even at ninety, my Mother continued to be the most determined woman I've ever known. That determination was used on my behalf more times than I could ever relate.

Those Nuns were all God-fearing, Christ living ladies who had a marvelous technique for keeping children like me quiet in their classrooms. Raps on the knuckles with rulers and willow switches across bare legs accomplished a lot for tranquility.

They achieved peace but, still and all, I didn't understand how wine could change into blood and bread into bits of Christ's body. This all seemed disturbingly supernatural and I was not willing to let it pass without a question. Suffice it to say that I have never received a reasonable explanation from any cleric to whom I addressed that particular issue.

Nor has anyone explained exactly how Moses parted the Dead Sea. On the other hand, I did achieve an understanding of how water can be parted under certain circumstances. This came as I stood at the Bay of Fundy and watched the tidal bore in full flood and at full ebb tide. I'll accept now the premise that a storm could have precipitated the raging torrent but then reversed and parted the waters.

What this amounts to is that many Biblical miracles attributed to God's intervention actually were phenomenal but normal acts of nature which the science of the day was not adequately prepared to explain.

In this regard, I have never believed in the old saw: **"There are some things you just have to take on faith."**

I would like a nickel for every time a bank president, an elected official, a teacher, a police official, or a minister has said that to me. "If you just have faith, you will be saved." Horsepuckey, I say to this.

I've found I can live without faith if it means accepting a patent or probable falsehood. Conversely, I cannot live without hope. Take away one faith and I'll find another one. Take away all hope and my world will fade to dust about me. We grow and flourish so long as there is hope. When you tell a gravely ill person that there is no hope, he will surely die. If you tell him that his faith will sustain and save him, he will stare at you in scorn. Hope is the answer, not faith.

Let me ask one more question in this matter of faith. Do you think that if Christ had understood that his faith would become a primary cause of war in the world he would have acted as he did? Or would Martin Luther have truly posted his edicts on the door of that Church had he known this would become the primary cause of battles that would virtually wipe out Germany? Or did Mohammed truly intend to inflame the entire Middle East with centuries of wars?

Reluctantly, I have concluded that most church positions are not matters of faith, but of control.. Think about them in terms of organizations, not in terms of holy sites and reverently held beliefs. Worry about fundamentalism of all sorts.

In regard to the threat posed to civilization by fundamentalism and its cohort, organization, ask yourself a question. Since men are genetically doomed to die within a 'normal' lifespan, a lifespan which admittedly has stretched far beyond that of medieval times, shouldn't man created organizations also have a designated life span.

Shouldn't organizations die when their normal life span has been exceeded? Shouldn't their assets be distributed as they are required to reorganize into one or more new entities, each with a new life span, or shouldn't they just die if their natural usefulness is depleted? The older organizations become, the more like people they become. Their joints turn arthritic, their thinking rigid, their interests rest more in preserving what they have rather than taking new risks.

Time permitting, I may someday pursue this topic to its reasonable conclusion – that is that each generation deserves its own chance to create a world it wishes to live in. I am acutely aware that most of the children I know to have been born in poverty never had a chance to grow beyond it. Don't we owe each new generation a chance to grow beyond their roots.

Just as I believe we all create God in our own image, so should we each have a chance to create a future with which we can live comfortably. I don't call this 'utopia'. I don't think of it as an utopian vision. In my arrogance, I think of it as 'Yinglingnism', the self creation of a better world to come.

After all, it's my book, and I'm entitled to think as I damn well please. Or so I've come to believe.

In this regard, what do I really think is the most important thing I've learned over the past seventy years. I believe it is that people must try to think rationally and reasonably with regard to the simple fact that other people may see the world differently. Above all, a person must develop a solid respect for his own thinking. People need to think about and recognize the world in which they live. This world we live in today is not the world of primitive man. It is not the world of medieval barons and monastic thinking. This is no longer a world where conflict ever occurs in isolation. Everything that happens anywhere in the world is now instantly impacting to everybody everywhere else.

More than ever before we need to become a world aware society. Isolationism and governmental and personal movements taken purely in self-interest are no longer acceptable in either theory or action. Action without knowledge can get you killed.

Further, we must accept the fact that genius is not a function of either race or gender. The person who is the most accomplished in any field must he able to make his contribution without being downed by the naysayers who see only their own gender or the color of their own skin. We must applaud diversity not down it because of its mere existence.

PART SEVEN

END NOTES

A. BIBLIOGRAPHICAL CONSIDERATIONS
B. CLARIFYING NOTES

BIBLIOGRAPICAL CONSIDERATIONS

In theory, you should be able to sit down and write your own life history without doing an inordinate amount of research. The key word, of course, is **inordinate.** We don't live our lives in isolation from local, state, national and international events. We don't live our lives in isolation from our families and their events. In short, we cannot just narrate our own histories without placing them in the context of where we came from and where we've lived. *Therefore, placing yourself in context is a necessary part of writing your history.*

At the same time, you cannot relate everything you know or learn about your life, nor about the influences which have shaped it. Some of the major influences on you came at a time when you were not paying any real attention to their mechanisms even though they placed heavy burdens on you and your family.

Examples of this, in my case, include the Stock Market Crash of 1929, which occurred before I was born, and the Depression of the Thirties which followed. I have read extensively about both, much more so than will be reflected in the pages of this book.

What this infers is that writing your life story requires **selectivity.** You try to recognize and eliminate items which would be fun to investigate but contribute relatively little to the main story. As an example, there was a black owned club in Gettysburg which was called 'The Savoy'. As kids, we grew up calling it 'The Cotton Club'. 'The Cotton Club', itself, was located in Harlem land presents a fascinating story all its own. I found not diverting to a comparative discussion of the two Clubs to be down right painful.

A third consideration is the use of **inferential detail** instead of infinitely detailed descriptors. For example, the laying waste of the Palatinate area of Germany is extraordinarily important to German families whose ancestors emigrated to America in the late seventeenth and early eighteenth centuries and must be mentioned. But that detail would tend to obscure the facts of my own life and therefore needed to be severely, if regretfully, limited. I found that some facts about the Thirty Year War needed to be given, but that the horrible invasions of the Palatinate by Louis the Fourteenth of France seemed overkill, as were the equally destructive battles of the Spanish Succession.

There is always a need to provide sufficient verification of facts and events so that a reader may go elsewhere to assure himself that circumstances were as the writer has stated. Therefore, it is necessary to include some external verification. They types available to me included: photographs, newspaper clippings, and correspondence as well as statements from other life histories. Fortunately, **or**

unfortunately, I tend to be a packrat. Winnowing down my own collection was painful. On the other hand, I didn't want to publish either a photograph album or a press book full of clippings. I also decided to limit the formal bibliographic references to books I'm sure the reader will enjoy and those which I consider mainline resources. Out of a hundred or more books I surveyed in connection with this project, I list only 12. They follow:

1. Bailyn, Bernard et al, THE GREAT REPUBLIC, A history of the American People, Little Brown & Co., (based on original text published by D C Heath, 1977)

2. Garraty, John A., THE GREAT DEPRESSION, Harcourt, Brace, Jovanovich, 1986

3. Forward by Jacob Yingling as Pesident of Carroll County Historical Society, Edited by Joseph Getty. HISTORIES OF NORTHWESTERN CARROLL COUNTY COMMUNITIES, Historical Society of Carroll County, 1994,

4. Lake, Griffing & Stevenson, AN ILLUSTRATED ATLAS OF CARROLL COUNTY, MARYLAND, 1877 (Reprinted 1993 by Historical Society of Carroll County)

5. Lash, Joseph P.,. DEALERS AND DREAMERS, A New Look at the New Deal, Doubleday, 1988,

6. Phillips, Cabell, FROM THE CRASH TO THE BLITZ, The New York Times Company, 1969 (Macmillan).

7. Rahn, Claude J., Genealogical Information Regarding The Families of HORNBERGER AND YINGLING, and related families of Eckert, Lenharat, Steffy, Gerwig and Rahn, Vero Beach, Florida, 1951.

8. Rahn, Claude J., THE YINGLING GENEALOGY, Vero Beach, Florida. (A note on the web indicates that this is being republished in Butler, PA by the Mechling Publishing Associates after being recopied by Janice Yingling..

9. Brunner, Borna, editor, THE TIME ALMANAC 2000, 1999.

10. Forward by Chandler, Davie, THE TIME CHART OF MILITARY HISTORY, The Time Chart Company, 1999.

11. Weikert, Jr., Edward L., HISTORY OF THE WEIKERT FAMILY, 1735-1930, Work started in November 1922 and was completed in March, 1930. The Telegraph Press, Harrisburg.

12. Zinn, Howard, THE TWENTIETH CENTURY, A People's History, Harper, 1980, 1984.

SUGGESTIONS FOR THE USE OF WEB SITES

Searching for genealogical information on the Web can become soul consuming. Read the following and take the warning to heart. If not, you, like me, can be eaten alive by the very leads which seem most productive.

I quote the following because it is well done, details the work needed to produce a genealogical site and is directly relevant to our main thrust of research.

Extracted from: 'THE RICKERT FAMILY HISTORY' at: http/rikers/org/riker/.htm.

"My interest in family history goes back thirty odd years, when there came to my notice a short account of the **Rikert** prepared by **Edward M. Smith,** author of the 'History of Rhinebeck'. This created a desire to know something of my ancestors and from whence they came. It was largely the incentive to the production of the present work. My original intention was merely to trace my own ancestry for my own amusement and edification. This seemingly simple undertaking involved much research and resulted in the accumulation of a mass of material pertaining to many collateral Rikert branches and allied families. So engrossing did the subject become as the possibilities appeared, I was actuated to continue it. Since the time and means that I could apply to it were greatly limited, the hours had to be done in my spare moments, and consequently its progress was slow. Doubtless with an expenditure of these two essentials far beyond my ability, for which no remuneration can be expected save in the pleasure attending such pursuits, much additional material would be found. It was apparent that little was known of the early history of my family, and no small amount of the information received from members of the family was found to need revision. While the Smith notes embodied important information, they were incomplete and contained assumptions that proved to be wrong. My indebtedness for this valuable record of the early generations is gratefully acknowledged."

This web site now consists of 43 pages of detailed, downloadable, information. My interest in it is based on the simple fact that his Palatine ancestors may well have been in the same group which included Christian Juengling.

Like me, this author researched "family, church and public records and documents, wills, deeds and tombstone inscriptions as well as Bible recorded [data], and information derived from members of the family, data contained in correspondence, old newspapers, obtainable county and other histories, genealogies, manuscripts, etc."

Most WEB searches start with a keyword or phrase, e.g. , a family name such as Yingling, Eck, Bishop , Riker or Roop (Rupp). These lead to group searches on topics such as probable church affiliations such as: Lutheran, Catholic, Dunkard, Brethren, Mennonite or Amish. In the case of the above listed names any of these could have led to segments of the religious emigration from Germany in which we are interested. Because of the religious wars, the largest single group of emigrants from Germany was probably Lutheran, although many of the above could be classified as Anabaptists of one sort or another.

This search leads back to more names, those of church leaders such as: Simon Menno, Jakob Amman, Martin Luther or his chief theological opponent, Johann Eck. (This name is of special interest to me because of a confusion we discovered in Taneytown, Maryland over the development of lad about Taneytown by an Eck or Egg Family. That led to the discovery that Eck had been born in Eck, Germany, which is now called Egg, Germany.) [All of which will someday lead to a poem designed to be bad called "Would you rather be an ECK or an EGG?]

In dealing with the WEB, you can also find yourself confronted with documents in languages other than English. For example, I don't have time to explore the connections but there are lots of Junglings such as Burker-Wieland Jungling. My limited German says he was born in Thuringen, worked for Ford in Koln and is now some sort of official, possibly in Hamburg. But don't hold me to any of that. Unless I contact him and find he actually is a relative. And I just can't afford the time just now.

You can also get productive results by searching on words such as 'Palatine'. You will find there are Palatine ship manifests which list passengers by name. There are individual home pages for ships such as the Patience which made multiple voyages to America.

If I had to recommend a single place from which to launch an initial genealogical search for a German ancestor who came from the Palatinate region of Germany, it would be the website for an organization known as **PALATINES TO AMERICA.** They can be reached at: http://genealogy/,org/-palam/ or URL http:/palam.org .

For background information on the Palatines, the website http://members.aol.lcomm/ntgen/taylor/palatine.html offers a number of bibliographical starting points.

Another potential source of genealogical information about your German ancestors is The Olive Tree Genealogy which can be reached at: http://www, rootsweb,cim/-ote/palatine.htm .

Great Grandfather Jacob Yingling was born in 1815. He died in 1892. To my mind, he represents what Christian Yingling looked like at about age 55 when he was involved in building the Lutheran Church in Trapp, PA.

CLARIFYING NOTES:

Note One: **THE YINGLING NAME:**

I have found two references from researchers which indicate that the Yingling name actually derived from a Scandinavian name 'Yngling'. One researcher, Barbara Yingling Miller, attributes it to a ruling house of Sweden, 600 – 800 AD. The other researcher, Lee Wolf from Baltimore, has traced the Yingling version of the name to an Icelandic Saga called the Heimskringla. Mister Wolf's letter to my son, Steve, follows.

"Steve, this is the information you requested on the origin of the Yingling family which is compiled in a book of Icelandic history entitled 'The Heimskringla, by Snorri Sturluson. While a lot of people can trace their ancestry back to famous people, or Lords, or even Kings and Queens, few people have so lofty an ancestry as the Norse Gods themselves.

I have copied here for you the entire text of the Yinglinga Saga – the origin of the name is first explained on page 14. I have also attached the introductorys to the book, both modern and ancient, as I'm sure you'll find many interestingf points plus footnotes throughout. The rest of the book continues in the same style progressing through the historical flow ofl Danish and Swedish and related kings up to the time of Snorri, about 1200 AD.

Of particular interest is the link (footnote p. 43) tying in the Yinglinga Saga with the historical king in England's epic tale – Beowulf.

Being a person of largely unknown ancestry, if I could pick a family history, I could not pick a grander one than this.

If you are interested or curious, I was in Iceland in 1980 and have a copy of the Heimskringla written in the original Icelandic. If you would like a copy of this or need any other info, feel free to write.

Lee Wolf, Baltimore Spice

Note Two – Extract from **SNORRI'S PREFACE**

"In this book I have had old stories written down, as I have heard them told by intelligent people, concerning chiefs who have held dominion in the northern countries, and who spoke the Danish tongue; and also concerning their family branches, according to what has been told me. Some of this is found in ancient family registers, in which the pedigrees of kings and other personages of high birth are reckoned up, and part is written down after old songs and ballads which our forefathers had for their amusement. Now, although we cannot just say what truth there may be in these, yet we have the certainty that old and wise men held them to be true.

Thjodolf hinn Frode of Kvine was the scald of King Harald the Fair-haired, and he composed a poem for King Ragnvald the Mountain High, which is called "Ynglingatal." This Ragnvald was a son of Olsf Geirstade-alv, the brother of King Halfdan the Black. In this poem thirty of his forefathers are reckoned up, and the dearth and burial place of each are given. He begins with Fjolne, a son of Yngvefrey, whom the Swedes, long after his time, worshipped and sacrificed to, and from him (Yngve) the race and family of the Ynglings take their name."

Note Three: Quote from **THE YINGLINGA SAGA** or the story of the Yingling Family from Odin to Halfdan the Black

"Chapter XII. **Frey's Death**. _ Frey took the kingdom after Njord, and was called Lord of the Swedes, and they paid taxes to him. He was, like his father, fortunate in friends and in good seasons. Frey built a great temple at Upsal, made it his chief seat, and gave it all his taxes, his land, and goods. Then began the Upsal domains, which have remained ever since. Then began in his days the Frode-peace, and then there were good seasons in all the land, which the Swedes ascribed to Frey, so that he was more worshipped than the other gods, as the people became much richer in his days by reason of the peace and good seasons. His wife was called Gerd, daughter of Gymir, and their son was called Fjolne. Frey was called by another name, Yngve; and this name was considered long after in his race as a name of honour, so that his descendants have since been called Ynglings."

Note Four: **How did Christian Juengling get to America and when?**
It is mostly accepted that Christian Juengling arrived in America aboard a ship from either Rotterdam or England, but I have not yet found any record of the voyage nor the name of the ship on which he could have arrived. Therefore, I accept the detail given on pages 15 through 21 of the section concerning Christian Juengling in Rahns's book **THE YINGLING GENEALOGY.** Since the book is apparently going to be republished and made available for purchase, I will not repeat the pages here. If anyone cannot procure the book, drop me a note and I will send along a copy of the original text.

Note Five: **An Alternate Theory**
Against the Rahn pages, there is a counter-thoery which suggests that Christian Juengling was born in America as the child of Johann Yingling and Margareta Kuhn. In theory, Johann was in America as early as 1664 and Christian was born in 1690. That would have made

Christian 20 years old when he moved to Philadelphia in 1710. I have not explored this question since I was most interested in tracing my own ancestry to him through his acknowledged children of whom there is ample record in my own lineage.

Note Six: **That horrible trip across the Atlantic by sail**

I quote the following paragraph from the Riker Family History because it is one of the few I've seen which portrays the misery besetting the German emingrants on their voyages to America.

"Joseph Reichert, a native of Kirchberg, county of Marback, grand duchy of Wurtemberg, Germany, came to America in 1700 with a large emigration mainly from the Palatinate. With beginning of the eighteenth century two currents of immigration rapidly outdistanced all others in numbers, importance and amount of attention which they attracted. These were the Palatines and the ScotchIrish. The Palatines were so called because their original home was in what was known as the Palatinate, a section of Germany bordering on both sides of the Rhine from Cologne to Manheim. The position of the country brought it into close relations with the Reformation, and large numbers of the population became Protestants. War had borne heavily on the Palatinate, when, in 1709, more than 6,000, most of them Lutheran, left their homes and, passing through Holland, crossed over and made England their refuge. Many, being without means, were subsisted by the English Government (At Queen Anne's behest). Some remained in England, some were sent to Ireland, others to Carolina and about 3,200 men women and children to New York. While they were yet in London (actually outside the city in special camps) and the government was considering means for their disposal, in November, 1709, Robert Hunter was appointed Governor of the province of New York. Hunter proposed to the Government that 3,000 of the Palatines be sent with him to New York to be employed there in the production of turpentine and tar for use in the British navy. The proposal was accepted and the people sailed with Hunter from Plymouth near the end of January, 1710. The fleet consisted of ten ships, being the largest immigration to America in colonial days. Beset by storms the voyage was greatly prolonged. Living conditions were bad aboard the vessels, much sickness prevailed and more than 470 people died at sea. The first ship, the Lyon, landed at New York, June 15. **[having been at sea over four months]** The people disembarked on Nutten (now Governor's) Island, where they sojourned about three months while the Governor and his aids search for suitable pine lands upon which to settle them. About 250 settlers died on Nutten Island. Ultimately, the selected site contained the wrong kind of pine trees to produce turpentine and tar and the entire project was abandoned two years later.)

Note Seven: **THE STANTON FAMILY: The lives and times of one of Gettysburg's oldest families** (from the Gettysburg Times, May 11, 1989. Written by: James H. Allison, M.D.)

James Gettys had a mulatto slave girl known only as Sidney. According to the terms of his will, on his death, the slave girl was to become the property of his wife until her death at which time the slave was to be free. However, as both James Gettys and his wife died within four days of each other, the Gettys family became extinct in this area with one surviving son moving away, it is not known whether the slave became free on their deaths or not until slavery was abolished in PA in 1820.

Sidney married a black man by the name of O'Brien but the date of the marriage is not known. She had a daughter born December 12, 1821 who, according to the family bible, was named Getty Ann Snaveley. It is not known whether the child was born before or after her marriage to O'Brien, or where the name Snaveley came from, but possibly this was the name of the child's father.

Getty Ann at the age of 17 on May 21, 1839 married a black man by the name of Greenberry Stanton. They had three children: John William Stanton born in 1840; Sanuel M Stanton born in 1842; and Maragaret Catherine Stanton who died in infancy on September 17, 1846.

Very little is known of John William Stanton, as he is said to have moved as a young man to Dickinson Township in Cumberland County. However, a family bible inscribed and presented to him by his mother, Getty Ann, on April 12, 1946 at age 6, is still in the family's possession. The remaining son, Samuel Matthew Stanton, was a life long resident of Gettysburg and a veteran of the Civil War.

The dates of death and burial places of Getty Ann and Greenberrry Stanton are not known. Best information at the present seems to indicate that as there was no black cemetery yet established (Lincoln Cemetery) the dead were buried along what is now Breckenridge Street extended, often in unmarked graves.

Samuel Matthew Stanton married an ex-slave by the name of Harriet C. on October 3, 1873 at the age of 31. The family Bible states that they were married on South Washington Street by a United Brethren Minister. As the family home was a log cabin which stood on the site of the present A.M.E. Zion parsonage, they possibly were married there. Samuel had previously served in the Army during the Civil War and, though the exact dates have not been ascertained, his grave marker states that he served with Co. C. 3rd U.S. Col. Inf. And it is known that he received a veteran's pension later in life.

An interesting physical description of Samuel Stanton, given by his daughter, was that he didn't look like a black man. He was light and more bronze like an Indian. He had straight black hair and supposedly because of his physical appearance was nick-named 'Satin'. He was a handyman and a gardener all his life. He worked for many years for an attorney "Jake" Kitzmiller who lived on Baltimore Street at the former Weaver home below the Jenny Wade house. It was torn down for the construction of the present Holiday Inn.

Samuel and Harriet Stanton had eight children: Samuel M., Jr. – born April 2, 1872; Emma Amanda – born March 10, 1874; Greenberry – born October 19,1880; Eliza Louise Catherine – born May 27, 1883; Jacob –born June 15, 1887; David –born 1889; John William – born Feruary 17, 1890; died March 5, 1890; and Freeman Stanton – born March 30, 1897.

The first daughter, Emma Amanda, left home very early in life to work as a domestic in the Harrisburg Area and nothing further is known of her.

The second daughter, Eliza Louise Catherine Stanton, lived on Breckenridge Street in Gettysburg just a few feet from where the old family cabin stood at the present site of the A.M. E. Zion parsonage. She worked as a maid for the Ingersoll's in Philadelphia for many years. Mr. Ingersoll was an actor and Mrs. Ingersoll was the daughter of a Gettysburg physician, Dr, Tate. When the Ingersoll's retired, they moved back to Gettysburg and built 'Player's Lodge', where they resided on the Fairfield Road, now the present Longanecker home and still called 'Player's Lodge'. Eliza Stanton Johnson was admitted to Green Acres in May 1965 where died on March 27, 19711 at the age of 87. She is buried in Lincoln Cemetery. She had no children.

Greenberry Stanton, the second son, worked for some years at McAllister Mill; then left these parts and (his) eventual whereabouts (are) unknown.

Jacob, the third son, lived all his life in Gettysburg and died here in the late 1940's. He worked in Harrisburg and commuted much of the time. He had two sons, Samuel, deceased in 1974 and Arthur who still lives on South Washington Street in Gettysburg.

David, the fourth son, worked for many years as a handy man and a porter at the old Globe Hotel and later at the Hotel Gettysburg. He also was a barber and did hair cutting in his home. David died in 1953 at the age of 62. He had four children.

A son, Albert, also worked as a porter at the Hotel Gettysburg. (He) was killed in World War II. A son, David Jr. lives in Harrisburg and works in Philadelphia. Adaugher, Cora Stanton Clark, died in the 1950's. A daughter, Jean,died in December 1985 in Philadelphia. She worked for many years as a receptionist in a dentist's office as well as being part-time secretary to Joe Frazier, the boxer. He nicknamed her 'pinky' because of her very light skin.

Before we mention the history of the oldest and youngest sons, we should says that Samuel M. Stanton Sr. died April 18, 1912 at the age of 70. His wife, Harriet, lived until August 17, 1934. Both are buried in Lincoln Cemetery, of which Samuel was one of the founders. The old original burial records of this cemetery as well as a chair said to have belonged to James Gettys have been passed down through the family and are still in the possession of members of the family.

Freeman Stanton, the youngest son of Samuel M. Stanton, lived in Gettysburg where he married Louise Palm in 1917. They had two daughters: Dorothy Harriet Stanton born May 28, 1918 and Catherine Louise Stanton born January 31, 1921. However, Freeman died in 1924 at the age of 27, supposedly from the effects of having been "gassed" in World War I. A year later, in 1925, Freeman's widow Louise married Freeman's oldest brother, Samuel M. Stanton Jr.

Samuel M. Jr., the oldest son of Samuel and Harriet worked for a time at McAllister's Mill, and then joined the Armed Forces. He is said to have served first a 'hitch' in the Calvary, and then to have joined the Navy where he served 30 years. Upon his discharge, he returned to Gettysburg where he married his brother's widow. For a time he ran the 'Savoy' taproom which was at the site of the old Dorsey-Stanton Legion Post on West High Street. For several years he was also the organizer and marshal of an annual Black Memorial Day parade. Programs and pictures of these are still in the family's possession. On May 4, 1937 he became one of Gettysburg's 'unsolved murders' when he was killed in a gambling game, supposedly by a white man, and which took place on West High Street. He is buried in the National Cemetery.

His widow, Louise, died June 7, 1985 at the age of 83. Her oldest daughter, Dorothy Harriet Stanton Carter, also died in 1985. Her youngest daughter, Catherine Louise Stanton Carter, still lives on South Washington Street in Gettysburg.

Dorothy had one daughter, Donna Jayne, who lives in Maryland. Catherine had two sons: Jesse and Jerome. One lives in Virginia and one in Massachussetts.

Thus have we traced six generations of Gettysburg's oldest family.

Note Eight: **Delegate Delivers Lincoln Tribute in 1970**
(The following article appeared in the Carroll County Times on February 21, 1999. It was written by Jay Graybeal, Director, The Historical Society of Carroll County)

Each year the Maryland House of Delegates honors President Abraham Lincoln's memory with a speech presented by a delegate. After listening to last year's speech delivered by Del. Joe Getty, I learned that Del. Jacob M. Yingling made the speech in 1970. The speech was printed in the Legislature's *Journal of Proceedings.*

"Lincoln Day Address to Maryland Legislature by Jacob M. Yingling , (Republican) Carroll County)

"It is an easy drive from Carroll County to Gettysburg, one that I often make since I have a son in college there. Many times we've strolled among the circling stones marking the dead and the damned of that Battle of Gettysburg; moved by the inherent beauty of that spot, by the verdant sweeping of the trees, and by the overwhelming feeling of American history.

There is the battle in 1863 to be considered at Gettysburg; the inevitable questions of its rights and its wrongs; of the failures of commanders and of men, of the deeds of heroes on both sides. Above all there is Abraham Lincoln's classic address.

"I defy you to stand on the spot where Mr. Lincoln spoke and not quote, at least to yourself, '...four score and seven years ago...' The words of his speech were few, only 10 sentences in all, but his earnest phrases have been impressed on our national conscience.

"Less well known are the closing words of President Lincoln's first inaugural address... 'In your hands, my dissatisfied fellow countrymen, and not in mine, are the momentous issues of the Civil War. The Government will not assail you. You have no conflict without being yourselves the aggressors. You have no oath registered in Heaven to destroy the government, while I have a most solemn one to preserve, protect and defend it. I am loath to close. We are not enemies but friends. We must not be enemies. Though passion may have strained, it must not break, the bonds of affection. The mystic chords of memory, stretching from every patriotic grave to every living heart and hearthstone all over this broad land, will yet swell the chorus of the Union when again touched, as surely they will be, by the better angels of our nature.

"After you stand at Gettysburg, you know that a lesser man, a man with less feeling for the American tradition, a less human man could not have held the nation together.

"Scholars have debated how Lincoln came to Gettysburg. They have dissected his learning years; studied the impact of his parents on his beliefs; traced the genesis of his thoughts to their literary endings;

and identified the traditions which gave him the strength to hold a firm line against the temporizers and equivocators.

"There seems to me to be three clues to the man's art of leadership. First, the reading of his youth, the five faithful companions as they are called, 'Aesop's Fables, 'Weem's Life of Washington', 'Robinson Crusoe', 'Pilgrim's Progress', and the King James Bible, are moral and traditional in nature.

"Another clue is found in a statement of O. H. Browning, a lawyer who knew Lincoln well. He said 'Lincoln was always a learner, and in that respect, the most notable man I have ever seen. I have known him for 10 years and every time I meet him I find him much improved. He is now about 40 years old. I knew him at 30 and every time I have seen him I have observed extraordinary improvements. Most young men have finished their education, as they say at 25, but Lincoln is always a learner.'

"Third, the young Lincoln picked up what bits of knowledge he could from listening to grown-ups talk. A lanky silent lad, he kept his ears open while his elders visited in the local store, tagging along with his father, he absorbed every bit of conversation among the older men. However, he hated gobbledygook and in later years was to complain, 'Among my earliest recollections I remember how, when as a mere child, I used to get irritated when anybody talked to me in a way I couldn't understand. I do not think I ever got angry at anything else in my life; but that always disturbed my temper and has ever since.'

"There are three great forces to remember: first, the impact of an in depth study of traditional and morally inspiring literature; second, a questioning mind broadened by a continuous and expanding educational experience; and third, the impact of adult opinion and action. He was a plain spoken man and wished everyone were.

"Mr. Lincoln was the product of adult example, of his own questioning mind, and of exposure to a tradition which caught and inspired his youthful imagination.

"In some ways we are in a time of questioning as turbulent as the pre-Civil War days. We hear that we are not relevant to youth if we are over 30; we say that youth does not understand money because these young people did not grow up in the Depression; there are increasing questions about the morality of work; the pressures toward a welfare dominated state mount every day. Middle class virtue is 'square'; the dignity of the individual and the quality of his life are under constant assault.

"Can we learn from this great man Lincoln? Or shall we continue the abandonment of our traditions to the point where our youth has no moral code to live by? Shall we permit our leaders and our institutions to refuse to accept the responsibility of giving our searching youths the limits needed to restrict the activities to reasonable bounds? Shall we refuse to exercise the judgment and restraint in our personal lives that could give our children a guide to grow by?

It seems to me that the lore of Abraham Lincoln clearly shows how a youth is shaped into a man by the forces of his family, his education, and his belief in moral traditions.

"The lessons of Lincoln and Gettysburg are twofold. Leaders have an obligation. They have accepted a responsibility and that responsibility requires the setting of limits as well as the establishment of opportunity. A leader, whether a legislator, a military commander, a businessman, or simply the head of a family, has accepted the responsibility to set an example for his people.

"Mr. Lincoln understood and accepted his responsibilities to set limits and to be an example. Any legislation which permits or encourages the abdication of personal leadership responsibility is not in the Lincolnian Republican tradition..

"Also, we must find ways to foster continuing education as a way of life for our youth. By integrity and by legislation we will find ways to promote our sixteenth president' pattern of personal growth to supply our leadership in the difficult days ahead.

"Let us adopt the moral fiber of Abraham Lincoln. His party leaders were afraid his stand on slavery in the senatorial election of 1856 would cost him the election. He steadfastly refused to change his 'house divided' statement. That expression is a truth for all human experience; 'a house divided against itself cannot stand'. "This proposition is true and has been for 6,000 years. I want to use some universally known figure expressed in simple language, that may strike home to men in order to raise them up to the peril of the time. I do not believe I would be right in changing or omitting it. I would rather be defeated with this expression in the speech, and uphold it and discuss it before the people, than be victorious without it.

"Let us stand with Lincoln at Gettysburg and know '...that this nation under God, shall have a new birth of freedom and that government of the people, by the people, for the people, shall not perish from the earth.'"

Del. Yingling's speech was delivered during the social upheaval that defined the late 1960's in America, including Carroll County. The impact of that turbulent era can still be seen in social movements, education and politics.

Jay Graybeal is director of the Historical Society of Carroll County

NOTE NINE: **PRESS COVERAGE: legislative years**

There is no justification for my inflicting the hundreds of press stories generated during my time in the legislature on the reader. I have more clippings from the Maryland and Carroll County press than anyone needs to read. Certainly, there is no justification in my inflicting them on the reader of this book. Therefore, I will merely list those which reported my position(s) on certain major issues. I believe the most important thing the articles can do is provide the reader with some idea of the fantastic scope of issues confronting our legislators on any given day. If our delegates and senators don't read fast, retain well, manage detail with aplomb and always show up for votes, they will fail in their duties.

AN INDICATIVE INDEX OF MY ACTIVITIES AS THE PRESS REPORTED THEM:

Del. Yingling bucks repeal of Ober Law: (The Ober law required that state employees, including teachers take an oath that they are not engaged in subversive activities. At the same time I opposed House Bill 80 which would have ended capital punishment in Maryland.

Yingling Bill Would Aid Fire Company Workers: "House Bill 511" said Mr. Yingling, "will permit Carroll County fire companies to bring their paid employees under State worker's compensation."

Need to Raise Property Tax Questioned: I was alone among the other members of the delegation in questioning this move being attempted by the County Commissioners.

Yingling Renews Query of 'Slots' Revenue Loss: In my opinion eliminating this source of revenue which is critical to four counties would be improper without first at least outlining how this critical income could be replaced.

Seat Belts Save Lives: With regard to the enactment of a seat belt law, House Resolution 71, I was quoted as saying "We believe, as we have said here before, that seat belts are the best insurance against injury and possible death in case of accident."

Checking up on Drivers: I had introduced a bill requiring re-examination of drivers every five years.

Dulany, Yingling Vote For Tax Boost; Weant, O'Farrell, Magin Oppose Bill: As the headline called it, the Carroll County Delegation disagreed on giving Governor Tawes their support.

Yingling Appointed to State Tourism Committee of The Legislative Council of Maryland: I was one of two legislators appointed to study the future of tourism and its economic values to Maryland.

Del. Yingling Questions Cooper- Hughes Tax Bill: This bill was designed to change the tax structure of the State of Maryland in order to help Baltimore City and other metropolitan areas. I thought it was unfair to Carroll County and submitted an amendment which basically pointed this out and placed remedies in place.

J. Yingling Backs Plans For College: "I personally support the idea of the community college and will do all I can to work toward the eventual establishment of such an institution in Carroll County."

Legislator To Be Women's Speaker: "Drawing upon his experience as a member of the ways and means committee, education and motor vehicle committees, Del. Yingling will discuss the role of women in politics." Legislators are in constant demand to address all types of community organizations. "Delegate Yingling, as Chairman of the speaker's bureau for the Maryland World's Fair Committee, has addressed audiences throughout Maryland."

Del. Yingling Given Credit
NEW INDUSTRY IN CARROLL (Carroll County Times)

Carroll County has a new industry and a lot of the credit goes to one of its young members of the House of Delegates.

The industry is the $3.6 million Random House book distribution center.

Construction will begin soon on an 85-acre tract about one mile north of Westminster off Rte. 31.

The young man who played a big behind the scenes role in bringing it there is Del. Jacob M. Yingling who lives about a mile from the site.

In addition to serving the County as a delegate, Yingling works as an area sales manager for the L. W. Singer Co., the textbook division of Random House.

His role in getting Random House interested in Maryland and Carroll County and the State and County interested in Random House was given credit by his boss, columnist and television personality, Bennett Cerf, yesterday.

Mr. Cerf is president of Random House, one of the world's six largest publishing houses.

"I don't think we would have come here if it hadn't been for Mr. Yingling." Mr. Cert said just after he signed a contract in the presence of Gov. Tawes formalizing the agreement to build the new facility.

"He certainly pointed us in this direction and we found he was right. It's the best place we could have found." He added.

A Delegate's Contribution (Baltimore News American, 3/27/65)

It is heartening to learn that the Random House decision to establish its $3.6 million book distribution in Carroll County was brought about in considerable part by one of its members in the House of Delegates, Jacob M. Yingling.

As an area sales manager for the book publishing company's textbook division, Del Yingling apparently believes that he should act in the best interests of his employer. And, as an elected official, he apparently believes also that he has a responsibility to his constituents.

Both viewpoints are refreshing in an era which seems to have spawned a pervasive philosophy of "what's in it for me."

Even should he fail to achieve sponsorship of any major legislation for the State or Carroll County betterment, Del. Yingling may find that his constituents will note the tangible evidence – in the form of payrolls – of his interest in his county when the next election rolls around.

Deaf Witnesses Subject of Bill: "The Yingling Bill" – calls for providing interpreters for court witnesses who suffer deafness or any other handicap that impairs his ability to understand the English language or to communicate.

Pay as you go – Down: A lengthy editorial in the Carroll County Times protesting the County Commissioners "pay as you go" plan for school Construction. I supported instead a planned program of bonded indebtedness. The Editorial ended thusly: "We earnestly believe that such a fund is direly needed. We believe that rather than poor economy, it is sound economy to reach, as Delegate Yingling put it, a happy medium in bonded indebtedness in order to have the money ready to buy new school sites and to build new schools. Those who shun this path because they are reluctant to pass on debts to their children should think of this: The burden of an inferior education is going to be far worse."

Fulltime State's Attorney: An editorial in the Carroll County Times. "Del. Jacob M. Yingling's plan to submit legislation establishing a fulltime State's attorney and a full time county attorney for Carroll County is sound. We believe it will be much more efficient than the present part time setup and will eliminate possible conflicts of interest that can arise under this system."

Change to be Sought in Bus Flasher Law: A member of the legislature, Del. Jacob M. Yingling, said today he probably will seek a change in a state law which bans use of red safety flashers on privately-chartered buses carrying children. (This followed an incident in which my son, Randy, was riding with another boy who was struck and killed by a passing car while alighting from a YMCA camp bus near Westimisnter.)

Plans for New County Jail Draw Hot Tiff: New-American Carroll County Edition, 12/26/66 The proposal was submitted by Commissioner Bair who said his "plan for the jail would mean the county would pay a lower total amount for the facility." "Yingling attacked the plan as adequate only for present needs with little or no provision for expansion, and termed it 'pennywise and pound foolish.'

Stop Conflict of Interest: The Times supports a strict conflict-of-interest law and applauds Delegate Yingling for announcing that he will introduce one in the present General Assembly, then reintroduce it for application to Carroll County if it fails to pass on a statewide basis.

Yingling Preparing 8 Bills: The first eight bills, said the Carroll Delegate will cover conflict of interest, school bus flasher lights, aid for the mentally retarded, midnight curfew on drivers 17 and under, legislation for the deaf, allowing county commissioners to purchase equipment over $1,000 without a bid in the event of emergency, and provision in school budget for transportation of children that are now being transported but not shown in the budget.

Naming of Study Panel Big Issue: A 'blistering verbal battle' followed a public meeting on code home rule last night after four officials 'unofficially' named a 21 man government study commission. The so-called battle was over who got to appoint which people could serve on the commission. My position was: "We want this committee to be impartial above all else." "We want to pick the committee on the basis of qualifications, not political views." "We don't want to pick a man because he was for or against the constitution or because he's Democratic or Republican."

State's Attorney Conflict Bill Has Merit: Delegate Jacob M Yingling's announced intention to introduce legislation that would prohibit the State's attorney here from representing any governmental agency as a part of his private law practice is sound. We hope he draws up such a measure soon.

A View of County's Delegation to Annapolis: Special praise goes to Delegate Jacob M. Yingling, who as usual submitted the most bills and, in this writer's judgment, the best bills. It was Yingling, as one school observer mentioned this week, who insured that Carroll County gets kindergartens next year (a move was on to have a phase-in program for counties now without kindergartens, of which there are 7 in the state. Jake stopped it.)

Director of Finance Bill Passed by House: A bill creating the office of Director of Finance of Carroll County was passed in the House of Delegates in Annapolis Tuesday. The bill was introduced by Delegate Jacob M. Yingling.

Juvenile Bill Passes House: Yingling's bill provided protection to juveniles against adults who have contributed to their delinquency. Governor Mandel veto'd it on a question of constitutionality.

Yingling Pulls Out Of District Congress Race: (3/13/72) "I would be very honored to be elected to Congress," Yingling said, "But right now time would not permit it. There are many things equally high on my list of priorities, things as important to me now as running for Congress." He referred to his business commitments, personal reasons and projects he has initiated as a General Assembly Delegate.

MISCELLANEOUS COMMENTS AND NOTES

I was in Aspers, PA, the town of my birth, taking pictures the other day. When I drove back out to the highway I remembered that the road facing me from across the Carlisle Road led to Bendersville. That was where Doctor Byron C. Jones who delivered me on September 30, 1930 had lived and worked for over 50 years. The tile works where my father had worked is now completely gone, but otherwise not much as changed in Aspers. The home where I was born still remains and is still in good repair. The rail tracks which lead from Gettysburg remain. At the time of my birth, my father's father was able to ride the train from Gettysburg to Aspers and visit my family. I felt a twinge of regret as I remembered that in those days you could also take a train from my current home in Westminster directly to Baltimore. Now, many people in Westminster don't want the mass transit rail tracks completed to Westminster for fear it will encourage a mass migration of urban 'undesirables' into town. (Whatever 'undesirables' means to the opposition!)

It is a bit odd to see that nothing much in Aspers or its surrounding fields has changed during my first seventy years. For the record, Doctor Jones died at age 92 after spending just one year in a nursing home.

In the same context, the Doctor who delivered my sons, Steve and Randy, died in 1985 after serving as a physician in Gettysburg for thirty years. This was Dr. David C. Stoner. On the same day I took pictures in Aspers, I shot a few in Gettysburg, These include former homes, as well as the courthouse wall where my father and I had sat all those years before. Unlike Aspers there have been significant changes in Gettysburg. The Courthouse remains but 'my' high school has been replaced by a mammoth new edifice outside of town. The current Mayor of the town is a friend from my youth and the head of the historical society taught me a course in political science before he'd even completed his Doctorate.

Two other comments relative to this return to my roots. Gettysburg College is expanding and no longer seems the bucolic college I attended. The old frat houses are still in place but the dormitory situation is changing fast. There are ever more fantastic schemes evolving to attract tourists to the Battlefield. When I think back over the early tales I heard of how my relatives lived near the Devils's Den and Roundtop and cared for the wounded in their own houses during the Battle and how the church at which I served as an altar boy became a hospital, the more I wonder if 'history' of the tourist type is really a good thing.

Is it possible we've become more a nation of voyeurs instead of a nation of doers? That is truly worrisome to me.